Different Strokes-How to Design Employee Reward Recognition Plans

Employee Motivation and Engagement

Dr.E.J. Sarma

Contents

Preface	*7*
Acknowledgments	*11*
1. Understanding the Workplace Behaviour	*13*
2. Workplace Culture and the Influence.	*39*
3. Ensuring the Employee Loyalty.	*50*
4. The Variable pay Myth and Magic.	*81*
5. Strategies, Design and the Policies.	*88*
6. The Employee Stock Option Plans	*104*
7. Leadership Influence on Employee Motivation and Retention.	*117*
8. The Most Preferred Employers.	*132*
Appendix 1	*143*
Key Concepts	143
Asclepiades	*143*
Appendix 2	*144*
Key Jargons	144
Appendix 3	*149*
Important Labour laws in India	149

Appendix-4	*171*
India's Top Ten Highest Paid MD/CEOs	*171*
References	*173*
About the Author:	*178*

Which is the one habit that every successful business leader like Bill Gates, Mark Zukerberg and Warren Buffet has in common?

Reading.

They admit that they are voracious readers and their die-hard habit is what makes them to be thinking before acting and be successful. These famous people do not attribute their success to luck or to their intelligence, but their thirst for knowledge.

The people who are voracious readers are always the leaders and most capable leaders are voracious readers. There is no better proof than the above great leaders. There cannot be better reason for anyone to read this book as the objective is to share knowledge on managing people and leadership.

The second unique aspect in the life of successful people is, to nurture a personal dream to accomplish something, very dear to the person's heart and experience the wonderful feeling of happiness and joy after realizing it one-day, and leave a legacy behind. That feeling is something which needs to be experienced and cannot be expressed in words.

Every professional must nurture a dream to leave behind the legacy of the experiences gained and lessons learnt through years of professional experience. The purpose of our life and living thus can become meaningful.

The best way to make the dream come true is to grab every opportunity while progressing towards the dream.

This work is my dream which has been realized through continuous learning for thirty years in understanding the human psychology.

Knowledge is a very powerful tool for any professional and can be acquired either by reading scholarly articles, good books and listening to talks by erudite scholars or through mentoring and coaching. Besides providing the inspiration, a good book works on the intellect by massaging it. Therefore, one sure legacy any true professional can leave behind is to write a book.

This book is expected to serve as an enabler in enhancing the effectiveness of every manager and leader who is vested with responsibility to manage people in organizations.

Students of HR, business leaders, decision makers, compensation specialists who architect employee compensation and reward plans can benefit immensely from this book.

This is one such attempt and the book will help those managers who have people management responsibility to be effective by gaining insight into the psychology behind the workplace motivation of employees through deployment of proper reward, recognition programs. This book can help to ensure designing the most effective strategy to enhance employee engagement.

In this book, one can learn about the good and the bad side of instituting the employee reward programs. Effort is made to suggest simple and powerful and low-cost, but most effective methods to enhance employee engagement many times over.

The book also lets the reader know how some of the great organizations have succeeded in implementing the rewards and recognition plans effectively and manage to be the dream company for many people.

Preface

There are two schools of thought on the subject of rewarding employees. The attempt and aim are to present both views -positive and negative - about introducing formal employee reward or recognition programs and other type of incentive plans. There is always a dilemma about issues like, having the formal reward or no reward, cash reward or non-cash, long-term or short term. When it comes to decision making on rewards these issues are debated hotly.

Every CEO in the IT industry I have interacted wants his company to be another Micro Soft or Google. There are few things when it comes to people management, which Microsoft or Google and a few other companies seem to do very well in creating the "WOW" factor for the employees. Of course, you need to make that kind of money to pamper people.

Many companies do not even seem to be able to successfully copy few of those low-cost ideas.

While trying to understand the reason behind this incapability,

I came to the conclusion that the differentiator is the leadership mind set and sincerity of purpose of the leadership combined with lack of depth in the knowledge about the psychology behind employee rewards.

Students of management in Business schools, especially those in HR specialization are taught everything about the intrinsic and extrinsic driving force. Using that knowledge, the HR professionals set out to prove their competency by initiating the new reward system if there is none or by attempting to change the existing system in the organization.

Is that an adequate success factor?

The other issue attempted to be changed by HR Professionals is the Employee Performance Appraisal system. Both these areas act as weapons of mass destruction, if not handled properly (metaphorically).

The way to tackle the obstacles without confrontation, when one tries to convince about the idea to the top management is not taught in business school as every decision event is situational involving multiple forces.

I had to face a situation every early in my career life, when the management team had created pay discrimination when it came to paying HR people. The team voted for a pay policy which would pay thirty per cent more base pay if they hired a fresh MBA graduate in the Software stream compared to what an MBA would be paid if hired in HR stream. Same was the case with rewards policy. HR staff did not have anything to look forward to by way of rewards. The game was set up for failure.

This leadership mind-set had to be challenged and fought hard to restore a sense of equity. This is an example of a huge inbuilt design defect in employee motivation. How can anyone expect the HR to manage motivation of others when they themselves were not motivated and feel let down?

The conditioning experiment conducted in the laboratory conditions where animals were subjected to reward and coaxed to repeat the behaviour, in some way had relevance to an understanding of human behaviour. The explanations for few of the complex human behaviour are no doubt the outcome of the study of animal psychology.

How far such experimental research on animals predicted human behaviour is only questionable.

This learning theory appeals to every HR professional for trying out reward programs without realizing that what works for animals does not work for humans.

There is also evidence in research findings with animals indicate that "increasing the intensity or level of driving force works up to a point, but it fails to keep enhancing the learning and performance". Even the application of the Yerkes-Dodson law developed in 1908 had stated an empirical relationship between arousal and Performance and described that performance increases with physiological or mental arousal, but only up to a point.

Unfortunately, the finding did not go beyond the laboratory. In the context of the organization and the work environment, every simple reward program can have much broader and complex impact on the individual and finally the collective behaviour.

Hence the need to get a deeper understanding of the subject of Employee Reward Recognition is *sine qua non.*

Acknowledgments

There are numerous approaches and tools for setting up reward and recognition for the contributions of employees in organizations. The dilemma is about the right strategy to follow and the right levels of total rewards that will attract and retain the best people.

Attracting and retaining right people are essential for organizations that want to retain competitive edge. Some research indicates that it costs the equivalent of six months' salary to replace the right person who leaves an organization. Designing smartly the rewards and remuneration structures that are competitive is therefore critical and cannot be relegated to back rooms.

In his famous book "The Fifth Discipline" Peter Senge highlighted the importance of the "power of acknowledgement". There is a reference to an interesting custom among certain tribal people in Africa, where the common form of greeting in the local language is the expression, **"Sawu Bona"** which means **"I see you.**

Each child is taught to reply with 'Sikhona' which is a powerful way of saying **"I am here"**.

The exchange of this type of greetings is aimed to give the importance to the person in front and not to show disrespect by ignoring and make them feel very happy.

This behaviour is equivalent to giving the gift of life and as powerful as breathing life into someone.

This African philosophy is my inspiration to write on this subject about acknowledgement of fellow humans I wish to begin by thanking the people who motivated and helped in realizing my dream of completing this project.

I wish to acknowledge all of my colleagues for triggering my thought process to write and complete my work. Many of my former professional colleagues with whom I had the good fortune to work with for over three decades and debate about the workplace employee motivation. I thank all of you for continued support and motivating me to write.

1. Understanding the Workplace Behaviour

In this chapter, we discuss the importance of understanding of the workplace behaviour of employees, factors which affect their motivation and the cultural influence.

Over two million workers are reported to be victims of workplace violence each year in the USA and over 33,000 workers are victims of non-fatal assaults on the job each week in the U.S. Between 2004 and 2008, on an average, five hundred sixty-four workplace related homicides occurred each year in the United States of America, according to the Bureau of Labour statistics.

Negative behaviour gone unnoticed has played havoc in recent years, resulting in violent incidents at the workplace.

Therefore, it becomes imperative to pay close attention to changing employee behaviour by rewarding positive behaviour.

The million-dollar question is about the reasons for individuals like Nasim who have no criminal record or intention to turn against the organization. She was very upset with the channel YouTube and was suspecting their role for suppressing her videos. She simply shot and killed three employees of the channel YouTube. Apparently emptying her hatred against the company policies and the management for discriminatory or non-supportive, non-communicative attitude.

In Florida, USA, an Awning manufacturing facility, witnessed the killing of five workers by their colleague. The worker was fired few months back in 2017, and he had a record of assaulting a co-worker and management did not take the incident very seriously

Though these may seem like the uncontrollable individual bad behaviour, it is time for responsible managements to deliberate about taking responsibility towards building a workplace culture of tolerance, mutual trust and respect.

The workplace culture has deteriorated, especially in industrialised countries like Japan and the USA.

Employee engagement efforts are ineffective while distrust in management is at its peak; Job satisfaction is low and continues to decline.

The financial insecurity coupled with mounting debt burden is creating fear and anxiety as the wage growth is stagnating. A very high percentage of people, even though covered by insurance, deny themselves treatment and medications because of co-pay issues and cost.

Stress due to the fear of lay-offs, longer work hours due to unreasonable deadlines, work-life conflict, enormous amounts of personal credit card borrowing and consequent fear are making the American work-place inhuman.

All the mass killings were the result of an unprovoked violent behaviour of motivated individuals who had some grudge or other against fellow workers or the management.

The organizations, therefore, need to pay quick attention to the unacceptable behaviour of the employees at work-place.

Managements cannot overlook their responsibility in creating a culture of trust and cordiality that could possibly reduce negative behaviour.

Many had shown signs of grudge against the boss who made unreasonable work demands or was pulling the rank and these went unchecked.

People indulge in bad-behaviour which *prima facie* looks very simple. Acts like leaving coffee in the sink or empty water cups near a water fountain, parking in reserved spots for handicapped or even leaving a messy work desk are committed by employees thinking them to be harmless. Even if co-workers turn a blind eye to such bad-behaviour, people get irritated and nurture resentment.

Examples of the workplace behaviour that create a bad workplace climate are:

Sex, race, religious discriminations and remarks.

Many supervisors not giving credit for the work. Lack of Recognition.

Treating people with disrespect.

Unreasonable deadlines and project completion demand by the boss.

Defying rules and policies like non-smoking, non-drinking.

Answering cell phones or texting during the meeting.

Late attendance to meeting.

Making unsolicited racist remarks.

Being the Non communicative boss or being passive aggressive. Communicating through email when face to face is required.

Negative emphasis on output.

Intimidating or Blame game by supervisor

Although there is difference in every manager's approach, the lack of the skill in communicating with team members, especially in giving performance feedback, communicating adequately about the rationale of unpleasant decisions or reprimanding a bad behaviour stand out as paramount reasons which are adding to the workplace demotivation and the weak hearted getting depressed.

Many managers shy away from giving negative performance feedback and many are only looking for mistakes and drawbacks in team members.

In a survey of eleven hundred employed people, that consisted of six hundred and sixteen managers, it was found that sixty-nine present of the managers said that they were often uncomfortable with communicating to the subordinates.

About thirty-seven per cent of the managers said that they were uncomfortable to give direct feedback about their subordinates on poor performance, fearing that the subordinate might respond negatively to the feedback. Every manager wants to hire the very best candidate, but when it comes to giving the performance feedback to the candidate, he hired the manager back out.

I was once asked by the CEO who happened to me my boss, to give the appraisal feedback to his executive secretary. I told him to do it in all fairness as the boss. He would not handle that as he did not want her to feel bad. He even used an argument that secretary is under HR and Administration department and hence Head HR should conduct the appraisal using input from him.

Managers are required to give feedback more often as part of job responsibility, but have to do it in different ways, especially in global setups where direct reports are spread over multiple cultures. Understanding this is vital to managerial effectiveness. In dealing with cross-cultural employees, the manager has to be aware of cultural differences, but there is no need to adapt.

When an air plane flies through a low pressure area in the cloud or even when it loses one engine and the plane loses height, the oxygen masks drop and the air hostess is simply trained to say that there is a small problem and everyone must stay calm .Imagine the behaviour of the people if the hostess says "there is a big problem and the plane lost its engine."

When the truant employee is to be told about bad and unacceptable performance or behaviour, a language like "kind of" "sort of" does not help. The manager's dilemma is whether the message should be sugar coated and softened when bad message is involved.

Confusion is created with people when sugar coated message is delivered in different cultures. When the boss says "think about a different way of doing, does that mean that I have to change or I have an option?

When an American manager tells his subordinate to change his style, does he mean to say "change or you will be fired?"

Giving feedback using language that can be direct while giving negative feedback or criticising is not usually done by managers for fear of being seen as arrogant but not in German culture. Reactions to the manager's style of communication differ dramatically from one culture to another.

The Japanese cultural norm requires never criticising colleague openly in front of others.

The French manager's style is to be passionate about providing positive feedback sparingly. An American manager would not do that, but would start with positive comments and then put it across as if it was a suggestion.

The cultural norms of working relationship must be understood for the right impact when the criticism is involved. I worked under an Indian CEO boss, though brought up in American background, would normally not use soft and politically correct or gentle words when annoyed even in senior management meetings. This was acceptable to his Indian colleagues, but not the Americans and many people left in short span.

Is managing the human motivation at workplace is a complex and difficult affair for managers?

The answer is yes. For many managers the understanding of human behaviour and comprehending the human mind does not come naturally, despite years of dealing with subordinates of all races, culture and ethnic background.

In my entire career, spanning four decades, I have not come across a single management team that has not spent hours of meeting time in discussing the issue of lack of engagement and inspiration to perform at peak by employees. Everyone in top management team feels that despite every attempt to elicit the loyalty and commitment at the desired level, the result is not reflecting management's intentions.

The issue of employee motivation appears to be complex, despite the wish by managers and leaders.

Psychological Research studies have provided adequate clues to getting a proper insight into the subject of human motivation and one does not need to be a trained psychologist to understand the motivational issues.

Very basic knowledge is good enough to sharpen the decisions on employee reward recognition policies which contribute to the most of the motivation or lack of it in organizations.

Rather than working on hunches and preconceived notions, it is worthwhile to rely on sound people management principles.

Some clarity of the concepts behind employee motivation and the impact rewards create on people can be quite useful for managing employee engagement and retention through proper design of strategies and policies.

Grasping a few of the useful and important concepts in motivational psychology can strengthen a manager's ability to manipulate workplace behaviour of the team members. Understanding how both intrinsic and extrinsic motivation works in a simple way can be the first step.

Business organizations have always a group of people in the workplace, who are hungry for reaching high standards of performance and are self-driven to grab the initiative. They perform above and beyond and such people seem to be in short supply while there is a majority who need to be constantly monitored, nudged, coerced or even punished to do what they are hired to do.

Human Resource professionals play the villain at times, indulging in labelling people as mediocre, average performers by forced distribution through the appraisal process.

Every manager tries to inspire the team member, but often gets puzzled and the question arises about the lack of motivation and the reason behind the failure of the team members in doing what they are supposed to do at an expected level of performance when they are paid.

Only a small percentage of the employees exhibit amazing devotion to duty mainly because of their personality and innate desire to indulge in that behaviour for their self-satisfaction.

On the first day of the new job, I had always asked the new employees' one question in the induction programme. "How big is the question mark about the company, role, and the boss and how long it would take for them to convert the question marks to one of exclamation?"

Invariably only one or two would reply spontaneously, saying that they had already fallen in love with the company since they chose to join after every due diligence. This exercise gave a signal about the company's brand equity and the gap that existed in management's perception and the People's perception

Intrinsic motivation:

Holy Spirit Hospital is a fifty plus years hospital and is closer to the place where I live. I have been visiting this hospital year for the past twenty years for my health check. The hospital can boast of a large number of loyal employees who have spent over twenty years and have been constantly adding capacity every year.

The hospital is always overcrowded and understaffed place because the number of patients coming in has increased manifold and the employees are stretched beyond the limit every day.

My recent visit was on August 2017. Whenever I visited the hospital, Philomena an employee of the hospital was assigned to take care. She gets assigned to help senior citizens, in locating various labs for the tests. During the morning peak rush hours when the other senior employees in the hospital lose their cool due to multiple demands and work pressure, Philomena is always smiling, stays active, helpful and is always pleasant.

A behaviour anyone will notice about Philomena is her high enthusiasm, energy level, the smile and high dedication to the job. It is a common scene in the hospital in the morning

Unhappy and discontented employees can cost high-cost in the workplace because they contaminate the work atmosphere.

They pollute the environment with their toxic behaviour, by stressing other co-workers, by lowering morale and the overall productivity. Consequently, even the employer is at times exposed to the legal liability.

The question worth exploring is how the employees like Philomena manage to remain insulated from toxic behaviour.

When I asked her during my last visit as to how she could manage to smile all the time and do the job for ten to twelve hours a day with the same energy, enthusiasm, day after day, for so many years. Her answer was simple. "I just love what I am doing; I like to serve people in need". Moral of the story is simple.

It boils down to the attitude towards self and others. To be happy in doing this kind of job, one must inherently be able to enjoy serving others.

If Philomena looked at her role as another thankless job, she would be the disengaged employee like many in the hospital.

Success for creating workplace happiness depends on hiring people with a happy attitude, especially for service jobs places like hospitals.

Managements can never succeed to induce happiness or buy it with rewards when there is a need for people with the attitude of selfless service. Happiness is intrinsic and basic characteristic in humans.

Let us assume that one fine day you decided suddenly started to do exercises to reduce your weight. It is because of sheer self-motivation to try it out on that day. This is an essential factor for self-motivation.

There are a few employee behavioural related issues every manager or leader need to know about workplace dynamics and motivation, this can be learnt without going through any formal education in psychology.

Well known psychologists "Myers-Briggs" and "Keirsey" had modelled sixteen distinct personality types, which define every human being. Hidden behind, this is either an extroverted or introverted type of person. The "Mouse" and "Lion" types coexist.

There is something basic about workplace motivation every manager must understand to shape team members' morale in the workplace in order to be effective.

The conventional wisdom is that by paying people well, one can get better productivity. This is no more valid. A research study at the University of Warwick established by making people happy, organizations can ensure twelve per cent more productivity.

The conclusion was that financial incentives alone cannot guarantee productivity. What else can be done to make employees more productive and happier?

Is it true that the brain works much better when one is feeling positive, individuals are better equipped to be creative and the ability to solving problems increases? Research has shown that when employees are kept happy, they are more effective in working towards common goals.

It is a great incentive for organizations to cultivate a happy environment that leads to greater levels of profits, by ensuring the future. Employee unhappiness cost 450 billion US dollars to the employers in the USA. Quite simply just knowing what is the primary motivator of each team member helps in creating a collaborative culture.

For example, when it came to picking up the most valuable the Airbnb employees picked the collaborative environment as the most valuable to put the company on top as the best in 2016.

Happy and satisfied employees will do everything it takes for completing the job on hand.

They deploy the passion to satisfy themselves and taste the success in whatever they do willingly. This is an example of intrinsic motivation.

Extrinsic Motivation:

Facing low productivity, the union representatives and HR manager of a glass manufacturing plant agreed to try out an experiment for three months.

This initiative was taken by HR because the majority union was suggesting overtime work and extra payments to get more finished glass ware into the pack and management was not willing to add to the cost. All the parties were seeing only the one side of the problem viz the money and extra work.

There were two experimental groups. One group was offered extra off time of four hours, if they completed 120% of their target within the scheduled shift time. The other group was offered an overtime incentive if they worked extra four hours and made 120% of their per hour normal targets.

The experiment was to get more production and find out what is more valuable to the workers. Leisure or more money? The outcome of the experiment was surprisingly different.

The workers in the second group who were working only for the overtime incentive produced far less compared to the first group who produced more within the normal shift time and that proved a point that earning leisure time is more valuable than money.

After experimenting for one quarter the overtime incentive plan was dropped. The proof is that when an employee is paid incentive to manufacture more, it did not act as a motivator and driver for action.

The motivation was more driven by what was valued by the individual worker. The psychologists may call it as extrinsic motivation. These act as a nudge that and can be extremely powerful when trying to motivate employees to deliver above and beyond their current comfort level of productivity.

When a manager thinks it proper to pay an incentive reward to a subordinate who has a natural passion to complete the task and go above and beyond, the effect is quite simply one of reducing the intrinsic motivation. That approach to motivate has an opposite and counterproductive effect.

For instance, in one instance an employee loved making the power point presentation creatively and was an expert. Everyone in the office took his help and he did willingly help besides his normal assigned duty.

His manager thought of appreciating and rewarding him, assuming that it would be correct to acknowledge his extra effort.

He made a business case with HR department to decide on some additional financial reward based on the logic that the company would have paid huge money if it had hired a person for the job.

When the employee came to know, he felt offended. He was not motivated, but it depressed him with the thoughts that his boss is trying to equate everything to money while he valued serving others.

Reinforcement:

The origin of the reinforcement theory can be attributed to Epicurus, who was a key figure in developing the theory that all good and bad emanate from sensations of pleasure and pain. The word Atomism originated from the Greek "Atomos", meaning unbreakable.

The theory postulates that only atoms exist, and there are no composite objects.

Epicurus the Greek philosopher was a major figure propounding the scientific view of atomism. In his theory of hedonism, it is held that pleasure is the only intrinsic value.

According to Epicurus, "the pleasure is in staying away from unnecessary desires and achieves an inner tranquillity (Ataraxia) that leads to contentment"

Epicurean doctor Asclepiades was first to introduce the concept of friendship, sympathetic painless treatment of patients. He was the one to advocate a benevolent approach in treatment. Epicurus emphasized minimizing pain and maximizing pleasure.

How true this is even today. Many managers in the name of control and supervision and task orientation inflict only pain, thereby destroying the motivation. Epicurus even warned about over indulgence which causes pain.

How many managers even today micromanage to cause immense pain to the team? The rewards are commonly advocated tools for reinforcement in behaviour modification.

The motivation is sustained due to internal drives arising out of pleasure experienced. Strengthening existing behaviour or modification is essential to make team effort more collaborative.

Change happens and lasts longer when reinforcement happens. The behavioural contract gets established through rewards that acknowledge the desired behaviour.

This is true both in child and adult behaviour

We all have seen that the teams under a particular manager always do better than others in organizations. Few of those managers succeed in encouraging the team members to bond well and achieve superior goals. Every manager expects their team to do very well without any intervention while wondering as to what can keep the interpersonal relationship healthy and happy.

The manager's ability to handle behaviour modification and to foster a collaborative culture through timely praise and reward is the major influencing factor.

Practicing to praise a team member in front of the peers after display of even a small contribution can encourage repeat behaviour. Social praise in public does influence behaviour while many managers are shy of praising subordinates.

Achievement Motivation.

Certain people have the unique endowment to succeed in anything they do, excel and deliver only the best.

It is not only this endowment, but self-perception about the skill and capability that drives the behaviour. Such people thrive only if there is autonomy in the work environment, adequate empowerment to assume total responsibility while executing.

Only in these conditions they would take calculated risks and set realistic but challenging goals.

American by name Russell Herman Conwell lived from 1843 to 1925. He was a lawyer by profession and later became a clergy. Conwell was tremendously influenced by a true story in achieving his life's mission.

The story was about an illiterate farmer of Africa. A British on a visit to his farm told him about the existence of diamonds in African farms and assured sure path to riches. The idea of making huge money excited the farmer. He decided to sell his farm and went in search of the diamonds all over Africa.

After many years of searching the elusive diamonds, the hope of making millions vanished.

Eventually the farmer was heartbroken and he committed suicide by drowning in the river. While walking his farm the new owner farm found an unusual looking stone which had extra shine and was about the size of an egg and he decided to put it in his house.

When another foreign visitor stopped by, the farmer thought of showing his unusual finding to the visitor. The visiting British friend told the farmer that the rock he found was the biggest diamond that had ever been discovered.

The farm owner had his shock of his life when he realized that his farm was full of those diamonds. The farm was the famous Kimberly Diamond Mine, the richest mine the world has ever known.

The old owner was literally living on top of ' Land of Diamonds' without knowing until he sold his farm to search for diamonds elsewhere.

Managers are in the middle of their own 'land of Diamonds' if only they knew how to find and develop the resource before searching the neighbour's land.

Every manager must remember that achievement motivation drives even the most laid back. It is about how one finds the diamonds in own backyard.

The motivation accelerates if the manager makes it a point to give positive strokes as the high achievers are always highly self-confident about their capabilities.

An important principle of achievement motivated people is a willingness to "Go the Extra Mile ". They believe in doing more and better than what one is paid for, and doing it with positive attitude. Charles Swab always performed above and beyond sincerely.

Carnegie hired him for that nature paid him a generous bonus of million dollars which was more than his own pay. The idea of five and Ten Cent chain store yielded Woolworth a fortune estimated at more than $550,000,000.

It was born out of the habit of going the extra mile; to sell every bit of old unsold stock in the store with an urge to put the dead stock up for sale at few cents. The hunger for achievement does motivate anyone far more than anything else.

Level of needs:

Maslow's Hierarchy of needs is 75 years old but till today is proving the point that human needs are never ending. According to Maslow the lower level needs are fulfilled only to be followed emergence of next higher order needs. Be it choice projects, Flexi time, fancy designations-there are numerous ways of rewarding to get people motivated.

Some experts call it moving away from a transactional contract to relational contract using the psychology. The hypothesis is that behaviour is not influenced by external rewards and reinforcements, but by internal needs and motivations. The implication of this model is that managers can shape the conditions that create employee's aspirations.

In the organizational context and work settings what motivates one employee may not necessarily motivate another employee. However, if Maslow were to be alive, he would have recast his hierarchy of needs to include WIFI as a basic need. In fact, Finland added WIFI as a basic human right now

Motivator- Hygiene Theory

The concept is based on the premise that any employee will have two types of needs. While everyone seeks job satisfaction it is the intensity of motivational needs that are responsible for satisfying when the work itself is challenging, stimulating, absorbing. By providing these, the satisfaction is enhanced.

Not that everyone can be given the job that they love, but even in mundane routine jobs one can create work settings that make people comfortable. It does not mean that by not creating interesting job one creates job dissatisfaction.

Hygiene factors if addressed would not result in unpleasant experiences and unhappy feelings at work and meeting the needs of hygiene factors motivates employees in their work.

Proper wages and salaries Wages, salaries and other financial incentives, establishing sound company policy and administration of the same, the robust interpersonal relations, congenial working conditions, job security, Quality of supervision, maintain the hygiene needs.

Motivators address the need to achieve growth. The presence of motivators ensures job satisfaction. Presence of motivators not only leads to job satisfaction, but also to better performance at work.

Few of the motivators are: Challenging or stimulating work, Opportunity for advancement, Responsibility, Sense of personal growth or job achievement, recognition are essentially the common motivators.

There are research evidences to prove the point that mere use of rewards or any types of reward systems have neither a positive nor a negative effect on employee.

Employee reward systems are hygiene factors.

If an organization does not have an appropriate reward system through incentives or bonuses, it may, at some point create dissatisfaction among the employees. This approach may not be helpful in improving its performance.

If it does have an incentive or bonus plan and can create successfully a culture in which employees consider to be normal practice it can create a higher-level performance.

The simple way for every manager to ensure motivation is to ensure constant job enrichment, which can maximize the potential of every subordinate to seek opportunities and realize satisfaction.

Effective managers must address equity needs which are the feeling of being equal amongst the peers. This is extremely important for team members when managers are trying to create high performance and highly motivated teams. The equity ensures the need of employees who constantly self-assess their efforts and outcomes of the job by unconsciously comparing with their co-workers.

Fairness in the treatment of every member of the team will have telling effect on individual and team motivation. Studies have expanded on this theory by classifying three types of behaviour.

Munificent Type or the hearted types feel very satisfied even when under-rewarded compared to co-workers and would feel guilty when equally or over-rewarded.

Equity-Sensitive type believes that everyone should be rewarded fairly. The feeling of being under rewarded leads to dislike and at the same time perception of being over rewarded invokes a guilt feeling.

The Entitled types disapprove if they are rewarded anything less than their peers and feel they have the right to be over-rewarded in comparison to their colleagues. The important point is that managers must keep a careful eye on the employees' perceptions and response with regard to rewards.

To be an effective manager set specific goals to measure performance, which can prevent the demotivation. Most managers try and avoid the trouble of spending enough time with subordinates to set the goals and explain the same in terms of what is to be accomplished and how the same will be measured, especially when the performance appraisal process begins.

The goal theory is based on the fact that an employee's motivation is directly related to the quality of the goals the manager sets.

By setting specific, measurable and challenging goals for every member, the team motivation can be raised and the performance will be at peak level.

While performance appraisal systems are designed with a provision to set clear goals, managers in real life spend very little time in goal setting.

Whenever the employees knew clearly the goal and performance expectations, there is no disappointment. People also elevate their performance whenever they perceive an opportunity for personal gain such as a pay-raise or promotion.

In other words, the employees who are driven by timely rewards for their work will decide to do everything to deliver the desired results in the future.

When dealing with status seekers, it pays to spell out clearly what is the changed level of expectation when pay raise, bonuses and promotions are granted as a reward.

Managers need to be the Pygmalion to manage the motivation properly. In the famous Greek mythological story, Pygmalion was a character portrayed as a king, father and the grandfather.

Pygmalion represented someone whose execution was always flawless with passion and was depicted as intense sculptor and misogynist.

In the story, his dream lady comes alive when he carved an ivory statue passionately dreaming of the ideal of woman. He fell in love with his own masterpiece of work and prayed to the goddess Venus, who brought the statue to life and he married her. George Bernard Shaw's then wrote Pygmalion as a play in 1912 which provided the basis of the musical drama "My Fair Lady" which was later turned into a famous Hollywood film.

The management jargon "The Pygmalion Effect" is about the self-fulfilling prophecy of the way managers might treat their subordinates.

When the supervisor or manager's treatment is positive on the expectation of the subordinate's on job performance the manager behaviour can influence and spur stellar performance.

As a manager or decision maker what can you do you to leverage the power of the Pygmalion effect for success?

So, you want to be the Pygmalion?

The leader must exhibit own behaviour that radiates high trust-based expectations to subordinates and arouses high intensity, motivation that spurs the passion in what one is doing

The Leader must also exhibit behaviour of nurturing, supportive interpersonal climate and must associate the subordinate's success to subordinate's personal causes and attribute the failures to external causes.

Leader motivates subordinates by invigorating their self-efficacy. "How does one create a self-fulfilling prophesy?" The only way is to communicate constantly with the team of the high confidence and high expectations in their capability and reinforce with timely recognition of every small step.

The benchmark could be to set high, but not with unachievable high expectations.

Support people in improving themselves to cross that high bar. Maintain constant assurance and not focus on failures or setbacks. A manager's own belief system on expectations of superior performance has an impact when he raises the bar.

The Superior performance of the subordinates is the outcome of high expectations of the manager combined with high confidence. The subordinates deliver on the performance expectation only if the manager is like Pygmalion.

Those managers who inherently have low expectations of performance are bound to get inferior performance. In order to make any reward program successful the role of manager's expectation that has positive impact on the performance cannot be ignored.

Another example is that of the Hollywood movie "The Dirty Dozen" a 1967 war film, which was filmed in the United Kingdom and featured many famous stars. The film was based on real-life group's story called the "Filthy Thirteen".

Though it was a work of fiction, it had a message in pointing out that the leadership with zeal and mission can work wonders with the team and the leader must have a good understanding of the things that motivate individual team members.

Learning the psychology:

The role of "operant conditioning" cannot be ignored if we want to understand the impact or the effect of rewards on employees.

Skinner's Operant conditioning experiments has the origin in the late 1800's and early 1900, an investigation of the disappearance of a large number of stray cats in New York.

The inquiry led to the finding that the cats ended up in the Edward Thorndike's laboratory.

Thorndike's would place the street cats in a cage and investigated as to how long it would take for the cats to discover the latch and set themselves free.

Initially, it took longer for the cat to escape than in the subsequent trials. Not satisfied with the findings, he did the second part of the experiment to see whether the behaviour will repeat in the future.

The types of behaviour modifications:

The concept of Operant conditioning is behaviour modifications controlled by consequences through positive or negative reinforcement or punishment.

A simple application of this is evident when you drive under the influence and the police takes away the driving license and levy hefty fine. This is to condition the repeated occurrence of the behaviour.

I recollect an experiment which I tried in one of my previous organizations to curb the late attendance by managers to meetings and condition them to come on time.

A rule was made that the late comers, even if late by one minute, had to put ten dollars in the jar kept on the meeting table and the meeting chairperson decided about the method to spend that collection. Something pleasant was taken away to curb the unwanted behaviour. It did work.

Classical Conditioning:

In this type of conditioning belief is that irrespective of what one does or prepares with response to minimize or enhance the impact of the outcome but the outcome will still happen.

The operand refers to the intentional actions of changing behaviour with the use of reinforcements given after desired response outcome.

When employees are rewarded for exhibition of expected behaviour, it demonstrates the organization's inclination to support.

If the employees also perceive such gestures favourably then, they are likely to increase their commitment, organization loyalty and even performance. It is the reciprocation process that initiates this behaviour. Similarly, an abnormal behaviour that was left unchecked or punished could lead to repeat behaviour.

The following example, may, drive home the point. The boss of an accounts clerk decided against a one hundred rupees salary hike. The employee was so angered and he perceived it to be unfair treatment.

He then swindled systematically one hundred rupee notes every month for next twenty-five years till his retirement. His successor found out that the employee had swindled exactly rupees one hundred every month and nothing more.

The perceived non-support from the organization also leads to abnormal behaviour. Skinner wrote a novel "Walden Two", where he presented the perfect society guided by operant conditioning principles.

Even in his work "Beyond Freedom and Dignity" which was controversial, he presented his ideas on how operant conditioning could be utilized in an actual society. Although the society was not willing to accept the Skinner's ideas, the principles of operant conditioning came into existence and are being applied even today in our everyday lives.

This revolutionary and powerful paradigm of psychology in behaviour management dealt with intentional actions that affect the surroundings. Solutions to questions in human behaviour can be found through this concept rather than in classical conditioning when attempting behaviour modification.

Behavioural scientists would remember Skinner as one of the most eminent thinkers of the time and the illustrious psychologist of the time. His view was that the driving force behind behaviour can be attributed to purpose through the experimental analysis of behaviour. Skinner reflected in his philosophy to issues of social justice. Skinner reflected on life after war during a casual conversation with a friend whose son-in-law was stationed in the South Pacific.

As World War II was coming to an end and when queried about post war life of Skinner went on to advocate experimenting and exploration as new ways of living.

Skinner's interest in ideal thought started from his very early stages and he had prophesied that sooner a newer culture would replace typical American materialistic ways of satisfying human needs.

His powerful argument was that "Either we do nothing and allow a miserable and probably catastrophic future to overtake us, or we use our knowledge about human behaviour to create a society and environment in which we shall live productive and creative lives and realize that without jeopardizing the chances that those who follow us will be able to do the same". (Not a verbatim quote)

The American society had the obsession for materialistic ways of living and Skinner tried to question that issue. The two components of Operant Conditioning are Reinforcement (or the reinforcer) and punishment (or Punisher).

Quite simply, with reinforcement one can increase the probability of a behaviour occurring at a future time, whereas punishment would decrease the probability. Sound understanding of these psychological concepts will positively influence the reward policies.

2. Workplace Culture and the Influence.

In this chapter, we discuss and understand the influence of culture on the work life.

Shantaram was born in a remote village in the coastal Maharashtra in India. He belonged to a community that was tagged as the lowest class in the Indian caste system. Like many from his cast, he could not afford to go to school as he was denied that educational opportunity. One thing all the boys from his village and community looked forward to was to become a master blower like the uncles and many male relatives from the village. That job fetched top end pay as the blowing skill was mastered on the job over the years under close supervision by working in a glass factory in Mumbai about one hundred miles away.

The blowers had to use the same gathering spoon shaped tool that is at the end of a blow pipe to collect the molten glass and blow like the balloon .To do this job the blowers would work only with crew members who are blood relations and are from the same cast as the stick is moved from person to person after a blowing. Shantaram became master-blower by working for over twenty- five years and he was paid five figure salary. The life time reward for the skill and extraordinary hard life is dream fulfilled. Many of them die of lung diseases too.

Shantaram, along with his relatives numbering about seventy, hail from the same village in Maharashtra in India and they all work as one crew gang. It is not surprising that the blowers had to be blood relations, as no one would mouth-blow into the pipe if it was used by someone from another cast.

Every day when Shantaram and his colleagues enter the factory gates, they touch the footsteps as a form of worship. I have witnessed two prolonged strikes which were bloody as the multiple unions fought merely because of the leader's ego. Shantaram and his colleagues would always safeguard the furnace and not allow it to be shut down at any cost.

They would stand by their ethics of not allowing the furnace to be shut down because they knew that if the furnace was shut down it would take four months to restart it.

For this reason, they treat the workplace is a temple and the work is worshipped. Such is the impact of the social cultural and influence.

The fundamental requirement in global organizations today is the ability for effective people management in diverse culture. That requires a sound understanding and appreciation for the work ethics in different cultures by managers and leaders who influence the individual and team morale at work-places.

Culture and its influence on work ethics.

Different cultures impose different norms that greatly influence the work life. In the culture of collectivism, the value of people and social acceptance are high compared to culture of individualism where importance is on individual excellence.

The **collectivist culture**, values the group needs of cohesion and working as one team. In the collectivist culture the self-perception is more of interdependency.

The collectivist culture is prevalent in most of the African nations. Collectivism places higher importance on collaborative task execution and focuses on what a group has in common. It will be futile to encourage or promote individual excellence in those cultures.

The fundamental truth prevailing in our life today is constant conflict about individualism vs. Collectivism. Does the life belong to oneself or to the society in which we live? The idea that the life belongs to an individual and everyone must exercise the right to lead the life as per own choice seem to be a myth.

Based on the premise that the human life belongs to that person there are strong manifestations of this truth. Individualism focuses on engaging in competitive tasks and the emphasis is on making the individual noticeable.

On the contrary, collectivism is based on the idea that the life belongs to the entire community or the society of which individual is merely acting one part.

In a culture that puts importance on falling in line and agreeing on social norms and treat jobs as interdependent, collectivism is more powerful, whereas in multi-layered cultures where affluence, independence, and differences are emphasized, individualism is very significant.

The culture of the affluent societies, similar to the American culture, which eulogizes individualism, always forces the members of the community to chase the "American dream". This is reflected in workplace behaviour as well.

Every new generation of American is conditioned to learn to survive, individually strive for a better quality of life and aspire to have a higher standard of living than the previous generations. The typical American dream is associated with all material things and comfort in life. Similarly, Britain, Australia and the Netherlands also reflect a culture of individualism. The French work culture is more influenced by medieval time.

The employee would consider a job as if being granted, the charge by the monarch and is under the protection of the King.

Unlike the Americans, French employees would consider layoff as an assault on the personal dignity and would seek the justice of the monarch.

The French people's working culture is more of a direction by principles of hierarchy, being traditional. As such, logical reasoning and high levels of analysis are the overtones of the work culture, which is generally slow and procedural.

A French employee values work-life balance more than any other benefit. The working hours were legally reduced to 35 per week and that had a positive impact on home and working life of employees.

The French working people enjoy and spend an above- average hours of leisure and personal care. They sleep over nine hours and spend over two hours in relishing a gourmet food. Their meals are twice as long as those of the average Mexican, who spend just over an hour a day on food. They have just eleven holidays and long lunch breaks.

They do less overtime work and taking work home or doing weekend remote work is absent. When you think of Germany, one can only think of industrial powerhouse. Germans have been super-efficient in manufacturing.

The work hours mean only work and no text messaging or use of WhatsApp, Facebook, Twitter and not even coffee breaks and gossip. The casual approach to work in the UK or America is not something that is tolerated by Germans.

The child benefit rules were revamped In November 2014 in Germany impacting the child benefit and parental leave.

The approach is to make child care more of a parental partnership. The attempt would make the number of working mothers to go up and increase the number of fathers working part-time and taking time off to care for children.

The reform was aimed at changing the family dynamic from the typical male breadwinner model to a dual-income supporter model. Many European countries look up to Sweden for the parental benefit and leave rules.

The downside of the work-culture is the shift with the lack of flexibility in the allocation of time for family life which had adversely impacted the birth rate and the

education of children.

Germans receive 25 to 30 paid holidays. Germany can boast of the most extensive parental protection policies and many European nations are following these policies. At-will employment is non-existent and all employments are contractual. The work culture is totally opposite of America.

All the Scandinavian countries are the most admired and least corrupt countries and earn the reputation of being safe country and the workplaces also have the same safe place's reputation.

Though the opinion is changing, they strongly believed that receiving government aid without eligibility is a crime.

They are safe beyond expectation. They do not have any safe room locks or security checks in offices.

Managements place a premium on teamwork and promote socialization. The unique aspect that differentiates the work culture is that no one thinks that they are better than another employee. Typically, they hang their egos outside the entrance to the office.

The Scandinavian society is homogeneous. It exhibits social cohesion, high levels of trust and a strong work-ethic.

This perhaps validates their welfare state in the words of an American employee working in India. The workplace culture is dominated by casualness and people often would say "will try, or will see" than saying no.

Lower level employees are not allowed to freely lead a discussion and are expected to obey seniors. This is in sharp contrast to American work settings. Indian or Middle East employers resorted to eight hours working style but everyone stays for 9 hours Efforts to improve productivity and make employees participate is carried through TQM.

Perpetual Guardian a New Zealand company tried 4 days week. Tree house a Technology education company has 32-hour week since 2006, which change move worked as employee retention increased, happiness, creativity, punctuality went up and profit also went up.

Asian work ethics are far different from that of American or European work culture. Work very hard to get rich is the principle that drives Chinese people.

Average Chinese worker spends well over forty-four hours a week. The work ethic is same in many East Asian countries like the Philippines, Indonesia, Cambodia Burma or even India.

The Japanese concept *wa* is about group harmony and conformance to social group norms and that spirit drives their management style. The work culture focuses on enabling and helping each other as a group and placing group interest above personal or individual interest.

They place less emphasis on compliance and focus on providing group harmony. As a team, managers rely more on consensus building (***nemawashi***), and even workers seek group approval for ideas before presenting them to seniors.

Group approval system restricts any individual not to be rebuked for mistakes. Reprimanding in front of others is considered as shaming and is very disastrous for any employee in life.

Chinese work culture revolves around collectivism. In that culture, respect for seniors and bosses, as a social obligation, is very important. The collectivist cultural influences the management style in China.

The Middle East, despite large-scale exposure to western culture and modern way of living, it has not changed its fundamental culture and lifestyle. Instead, there is an increased influence of religion which drives the culture.

A look at the Indian society reveals that it is divided. Forty-eight per cent of the population is individualistic while fifty-two per cent is collectivist.

Perhaps for the majority Indians, the influence and the driver are from the Hindu religious philosophy which is in many aspects similar to the African philosophy of Ubuntu (driving mutual respect and tolerance).

The learning methods adopted by some of the African cultures are worth emulating.

They teach children the concept of "respect for others" and "collectivism" from early stages. There are no parental conditioning and lollypop culture.

An anthropologist had narrated about an exciting experience he had, during his stay with the Ubuntu community. He proposed a game to a group of children. He then placed a basket of chocolates under a tree about 100 meters away and told the children that they had to run and the winner would get all. Quite surprisingly the children did not run and compete with one another.

They all joined their hands and ran together and got the sweets only to enjoy the joy of sharing.

When asked for the reason for their behaviour, they responded by saying Ubuntu (humane). The value system taught to them is never to seek happiness at someone else's cost.

The word, "Ubuntu" is from Naguni language and is from one of the Bantu dialects of Africa. Ubuntu teaching is all about striving to help people with the spirit of service and to show respect to others and be honest and trustworthy.

In both the Shona and Zulu language which is spoken by the majority in Zimbabwe, the teaching is common and always about a collective living *"munhu munhu nekuda kwevanhu"*.

Ubuntu is an African universal human brotherhood concept. Ubuntu is the potential for being human, to value the good of the others above self. There is one play-school in the north western region of India, closer to the border of Pakistan.

One can witness an amazing method adopted by the dedicated school teacher who receives less than two dollars per day salary as a reward for her life shaping effort. She had found out a unique method to shape the young children's attitude towards collective effort and to help each other.

In the playroom, the teacher had placed few colourful softballs that varied in size from smaller and lighter to bigger and heavier. She made the children stand in line and asked them to lift the ball one after another, starting with the lightest ball.

The children experienced initial success with the lighter balls, but faced difficulty as they moved on to the heavier balls until they were unable to lift the heaviest ball by themselves.

That is when all other children were encouraged to join and lift together the heaviest ball. The group effort gives them experiential learning of the philosophy to live the life with the philosophy of "united we stand".

This learning is something vital in shaping this collectivist attitude necessary for survival in a war zone.

Twenty-first- century workplace is much complex and different due to the widespread use of technology and the diversity of culture.

Therefore, the traditional, proven reward programs are not relevant to produce the enthusiasm and motivation.

In one experiment when people were offered enough money to live comfortably in their entire life, seventy per cent of those who had jobs showed preference to keep working than fade away. On the other hand, there were people for whom work was important, but would always look for up the ladder. The million-dollar question is what then is a good work or great workplace and how to create it?

During his business visit to a Japanese factory, my friend had a unique experience.

An old Japanese worker was seen sitting in front of the factory gate and he was happily removing the shoes of the visitors who entered the electronic factory.

When my friend they returned after his tour, he was thrilled to receive the shoes back, which were well polished and shining and the socks were washed and ironed. The shoes and socks came with a rose and three bows from the worker.

Out of curiosity, my friend asked as to how much he got paid for doing that job. The reply was surprising. He was doing an honorary duty to his employer, post retirement. As a gesture of gratitude for the employer who took care of him for many years, he needs to give something back and that was his way of expressing his gratitude. How many people these days would reciprocate like this?

Good work ethic motivates and even the most routine and mundane tasks are like the paintings of Michelangelo or Music of Beethoven or even Shakespearean poetry. The execution is flawless with pride.

More than fifty per cent of companies in the USA uses some form of incentive plan and spend over seventy-seven billion dollars annually on incentives. More than half of that is non-cash award.

Hefty incentives, paid vacations, birthday treat, theme parties, and plaques have been in existence as rewards based on the behaviourist theory of driving force.

In most of the manufacturing setups, output based incentives are known as "payment by results". However, the system has changed its shape in recent years and is known as gain-sharing or work team results.

Many forward-thinking managers who endorse team-work, participative management culture, continuous improvement efforts and similar ideas, support the use of rewards to institute and maintain these initiatives.

They use reward as bait to accomplish their own goals. Having experimented with reward systems in many cultures by introducing both monetary and non-monetary rewards it is my firm conclusion that either way you are worse off,

When you introduce the rewards with expectations to reduce voluntary attrition and if the attrition still happens to be high, HR is facing the management's ire.

If HR department does not introduce the rewards it will still suffer from the criticism from of employees for being very conservative.

The options must be weighed and one therefore, has to be very clear while taking any decision to introduce reward plans. At the same breadth, with drawing any reward also can be unpleasant experience if not backed by solid reason. The question whether rewards really are effective in the organizational context, needs to be answered before anything else.

3. Ensuring the Employee Loyalty.

Is there any management, which has not wrestled with the question, "What could be the best strategy to ensure the employee loyalty and engagement?"

Everyone is wrestling even today to figure out if it is the above market median pay, liberal health and retirement benefits, fancy perquisites, accelerated career progression or ample reward and recognition?

Above all, there are many focus on company culture, job security, job satisfaction, work life balance etc.

We analyse these critical management issues in this chapter.

The Employee satisfaction has to do mostly with the jobs and the role the employees play. The degree to which the job experience is emotionally stimulating, decides the satisfaction level. The employee engagement has to do with not only the job, but rises beyond to the organizational vision, values policies and the principles and practices.

The engaged employees feel proud and passionate about their association with the employer only when they identify with these ideals. The leadership has a large role to play in creating the climate of trust and confidence which ultimately leads to better engagement.

It may be worthwhile to measure engagement through 360-degree feedback as to how the employees eel about being valued, given credit for a job well done, the manager's ability to be fair and give proper direction and guidance

There could be numerous reasons for an organization to have an employee reward plan. Nonetheless, let us get this straight. Reward programs are neither a guarantee for ensuring the employee's loyalty nor a passport to superior performance. The reward plans can at best act as symptomatic treatment to achieve short-term and purely a temporary correction in employee behaviour.

Reward programs have not known to have produced lasting and changes in employee behaviour just as penalizing an employee's wrong behaviour does not prevent similar behaviour. The positive effect of rewarding lasts only for a few days, just like the loss of the swing and the sting of a cricket ball when the shine fades away.

Similar to many other rewards the trend in rewarding employees with long service after they spend more than five or ten years has been prevalent for a long time. The Millennials employees are comparatively more mobile. Today's generation believes that unless the resume has three jobs in less than five years one is not in demand. It makes no impact in that scenario to celebrate five or ten-year service as loyalty milestones.

The answer to employee retention may, therefore, lie in integrating newer employees into the organizational culture quickly and attempt to retain through the first three years.

If employees can be retained through the first two to three years the odds of retention for long-term becomes greater. There can be no better example than japan in employee retention.

From the unassailable status of being the world leader with a booming economy, Japan lost some clout and shine recently. Yet, the Japanese economy continues to have lower unemployment rate and higher employment stability.

An employee who puts in over ten or more years could be dead sure of job security and stability, unlike the American counterpart and that approach enables over seventy per cent employee retention.

The Japanese economy had a record level of economic growth in the last few years. During the last five years, Japan's economy registered the longest expansion since the end of World War II, outsmarting the "Izanagi boom" of 1965–70. Labelled as "Abenomics expansion" the economic expansion is predicted to match the post-war record.

The impact of the new surge in the economic tempo is, that young workers are now eager to switch jobs for better pay hikes unlike their older counterparts who believed in staying with one and same company and the job. Many young Japanese workers have never felt the security of lifetime employment that was common to the ageing older generations.

Japan faces the tightest labour market in four decades and tiny companies, food chains; restaurants are now hiring more Chinese, Nepalese and Filipinos. Japan has opened itself to low-wage foreign labour, though not in big way.

The foreigners are mostly being hired in low level jobs like convenience stores and it has been already opposed by the local bodies. As birth rate declines, there is a shortage of people to handle jobs.

Japan has fewer foreign workers than other developed nations, but the number is growing, which is one reason why wages are low among the migrant workers.

One third of all the migrant workers are Chinese, followed by Vietnamese and Nepali workers. Minimum wage in Japan is too low and does not attract many migrant workers.

Foreign workers come to Japan as language students and work up to twenty-eight hours a week. Most migrant labour work beyond the prescribed limit of working hours.

Corporate culture in Japan is to respect and reward the seniority. Since early fifties the compensation of employed people depends on the length of service along with a lifetime guarantee on the job. Companies could raise salaries as a reward for the staff's loyalty. The common approach is to offer a low starting pay to fresh graduates, who have to train on-the-job and work their way up. The average starting pay in Japan is still lower than the developed countries with similar economy. The seniority-based wage system also started to give way once the economy stagnated. Consequently, Japanese companies are planning to restructure, cost-reduction and, even the unknown job cuts.

The new age workers are opting out for companies like Cyberagent who have switched to performance-based reward system.

Accepting a low starting salary with the company that gave a break with the hope of lifetime employment is no more appealing to the younger generation.

A twenty-nine-year-old would take up a job with traditional company offering age-based compensation would not hesitate to switch to Cyberagent, with performance-based rewards.

The reward he expects is to speed up career advancement to be manager in nine years instead of thirty years that would have taken in traditional jobs.

New era technology company, CyberAgent could succeed to establish the new work culture, even though their managers had previously worked in the traditional Japanese company culture. Even they felt the old system to be unfair and hence supported the western type performance-based rewards.

Sony and Hitachi, the electronic giants announced the new system based on skills and performance and the initiative was totally opposed the change was resisted by managers who were not comfortable with performance assessment.

Fujitsu introduced the new performance-based salary system in 1993 but had to abandon it in two years.

The idea of lifetime employment and the seniority-based wage system is now being re-adopted by even Cybergate offers like a few days off for employees starting a family with generous and unique compensation is becoming common.

Cybergate innovated with granting even leave for those who want to visit a fertility clinic. Accordingly, the conclusion is that the cultural shift is now vogue.

The legal system permits wage adjustments when the economy is down rather than resorting to downsizing as it happens in the American capitalistic economy.

Japan may be the only country in the world where the probability of job loss goes down to zero once you spent long years in the company. Japan has been having the longest working hours and Japanese people work themselves to death. "Karoshi" in Japanese is a term that even describes the cause of death as excessive working. What causes the Japanese to work so hard and long? It is simply the phobia and their inherent inability to relax.

The declining job security causes many young Japanese to commit suicide due to stress and overwork.

When the Americans work forty-eight hours a week, the Japanese log in more than eighty hours a week and that is not uncommon. It is even considered bad if you leave before your boss leaves work.

The Japanese get twenty days of annual leave but forty per cent do not take this leave. Some local government agencies even switch off lights forcing people to leave work. The spending rule for this type of award is over US dollar fifty or one hundred for every year of service, while IT companies spend a lot more.

An IT services company in bay area offered to the employees one week fully paid trip within the USA for the employee with his spouse and two kids for the fifth anniversary and ten days of fully paid trips to self and family to specified destinations in Europe for two people after continuous service of ten years Many employees who dreamt of Alaskan cruise got their dream vacation.

The main disadvantage when committing to the service award with the intention to retain people is that it may look a lot easier when the size is smaller and the budget is not too stiff. It may become unmanageable when the company grows and headcount increases. Even these days, many organizations are blindly instituting the milestone awards for employees.

The truth is employers cannot secure a durable loyalty by rewarding the milestone anniversaries with liberal paid vacation or other rewards. Employees may not swear by a long stint just because they were rewarded.

By acknowledging someone's contribution with a reward invokes positive feeling which has a lasting effect. There was a reward plan to encourage emerging talents in one of the organizations where I was heading the HR function.

There were few deserving nominations for the award and it was a close contest.

The selection committee strongly felt that rather than to any senior employee, the award should go to the junior most eligible contestant. The impact of the decision was counterproductive as within one month of receiving the award, the employee was sitting in an exit interview with the HR manager.

The self-perception of that employee was, for his proven capability as the top performer, he deserved higher pay. He thought it would be only fair for the current employer to meet the competitor's pay offer. The manager who nominated the employee for the award felt offended and thought that the attitude was selfish and that had an adverse effect on the reward plan itself.

The top management decided to scrap the entire award scheme. The laudable aim of the management to reward superior performance and to get other employees to emulate the behaviour failed to get even temporary loyalty from the employee.

This is not what any management team would expect to get in return for rewarding an employee.

Any disappointment is followed by an unhappy feeling which drives the individual to behave totally in a different way and makes the person even do an act that is unexpected and untried things to avoid any further disappointment.

When one gets disappointed, the feeling generated is also one of emotional dejection. Disappointment is the outcome when the reward experience is not positive.

When someone is disappointed, the focus is on alternative outcomes. Think of a situation when a person gains some money in the stock trading. The excitement is short-lived till one compared and found out how the gains could have been much better in a better deal. The same psychology works when the employee rewards are announced.

The excitement of winning lasts till one finds out that another person from his group won a better reward.

Despondency and negative feelings arising out of unfulfilled aspirations to win reward can last longer. Announcement day of winners of various awards in organizations is the most stressful day, as it makes employees who did not make it to feel disappointed and sulk.

The employees who did not get those awards would not admit or acknowledge openly that the other employee deserved to win. When someone loses in any competition, the immediate reaction is to even doubt or question the whole system.

The bigger question or dilemma before the decision- makers is whether rewards will trigger better output if combined with a competitive spirit? What would be the effect on the company culture in the long run? There is not much of evidence to support these ideas while the opposite seems to be true.

The promise of huge incentive and intense competition, it generates, has worked as a deadly combination in many organizations resulting in catastrophic and fatal outcome for the organization.

The whole world is aware of the consequences of an obsession for winning at any cost as it happens in American culture. This intense feeling pervades in everything from war to sports to making it to the top of the corporate ladder. This obsession with winning has always had an ugly connotation. This has become, synonymous with greed, envy.

When one is obsessed with outperforming others and "win at any cost "it is damaging, because, like gambling in Vegas the odds are generally against gains always. When reward plans are set up with the goal of encouraging competition, it is a trap for humiliation, embarrassment, and demotivation.

The joy of winning is always short- lived as the most disturbing feature of competition to win anyhow negatively affects interpersonal relationships.

India's only female athlete P.T. Usha was running in the final of four hundred-meter events in the Olympic race. She lost the bronze medal in the Los Angeles Olympics by one-hundredth of a second and lost all the glory that would have followed, if she had won that medal, she would have been in the history books as Indian's first women to have won the medal in Olympic.

Did she deserve the lack of admiration even after brave and historic personal effort with minimal support or expert coaching? Such win - lose games raise a question, "is the divide between winners and losers worth creating in organizations through a system of huge monetary rewards?"

Just as winning produces ecstasy, loss generates agony, especially when it is a close finish. Derek Redmond was highly competitive and wanted to win the Olympic medal. In the summer of 1992 Barcelona Olympics, he was in the men's four hundred-meter semifinals. One hundred and fifty meters into the race Derek Redmond's hamstring tore apart grinding him to halt.

With his dad supporting Redmond restarted the run even with agonizing one-legged skip, and went across the finish line. Redmond did not have anything but a win when he arrived at the Summer Games.

He stole a place in the heart of millions of people since then, though Redmond did not win a medal.

The moral is simple. It is not the winners who are always remembered. To this day, people can't name the medal winners of that race, but everyone who witnessed the event remembers Redmond.

Many employees, especially the top performers, look forward to getting a reward, and nurture higher anticipation. When their expectation does not come true or fails, it results in huge disappointment and they become less productive.

There is conclusive evidence that people with anticipation to receive a reward for completing or for just completing a task successfully, simply do not perform at a superior level, compared to those who do not nourish with no anticipation.

It is the human nature to anticipate that drives someone to work towards the reward and make them deliver less in the absence of reward. In work-place people work only in the environment which fetches the monetary return for doing

something. The rewards destroy the creative spirit of employees.

An experiment was conducted with consumer product designers and the participants produced highly qualitative results without any reward for the effort and when a huge incentive was introduced the quality of output dropped.

This proves the point that creative people are determined to invent despite the absence of an offer of money. Their urge is to make the world better place to live in. Creative people do not work for getting the reward when involved in an invention.

By and large, management's belief system is that the carrot of reward for employees would keep the motivation level up. This is a myth and has been disproved many times over.

On the contrary, rewards have the potential to create distortions in pay and can sabotage the pay parity. Any monetary incentive has the potential to create huge inequality in employees' total earnings. Imagine the situation where a salesman gets a windfall order, which brings huge incentive in one-quarter. The way it can upset day to day rhythm of the lifestyle of that person is very adverse.

Moreover, such windfall gains create social and emotional stress in the family and the friend circles because of the temporarily elevated lifestyle.

The $1.5 billion Powerball jackpot winners or the winners of the game show "How to be a millionaire" reportedly been sadder and stressed after the windfall gain.

Many winners met with an unhappy life as it dramatically shifted their life to the top gear. The author of the famous book 'Life Lessons", had pointed out that terrible things happened in the life of his clients who were mainly winners of huge lottery.

Some even committed suicide because of the sudden upheaval for which they were totally ill-prepared for such windfall winnings which made their lives worse instead of enhancing.

The tendency of people is to go crazy with spending when there are unexpected windfall gains only to regret it later for being unable to maintain the same style. Rewards end up creating heartburns among peers and consequently attrition.

Expecting an employee to behave in the most appropriate and acceptable way with the promise of a reward in return is not really very different from telling the employee not to indulge or repeat an unacceptable behaviour with the threat of discipline. If an organization built a culture of rewards for every action, the employee's focal point becomes the reward itself than the goal to be accomplished.

When the motive behind the design of the reward is to elicit or encourage certain behaviour, it pushes the manager to be more manipulative with the subordinates.

That generates the feeling of being controlled and is likely to assume revengeful perception over time. Penalty and reward approach thus belong to the same family.

Both sides end up having a negative overtone because they are perceived as a calculated move. An employee who had worked harder anticipating a reward ends up feeling belittled which is as bad as being penalized.

The child in the person sulks and tells that "you got cheated". For any employee who worked extra hard, if the reward was not forthcoming, the psychological effect is always traumatic and depressing.

When the anticipation runs high for reward, it is more depressing and demoralizing from a miss-out. The dilemma of reward or discipline is always taunting every management.

Managers are tempted to hire subordinates who are more prone to comply and do things as per the manager's demand and the manager then rewards for compliance and expect a repeat behaviour.

This approach is no different from another type of manager whose way is to find people who are doing something wrong and disciplining them with hope to stop that behaviour. Both categories of managers live in a paradigm of their own. Either is not the correct approach as both are perceived as controlling.

When questioned about not nominating a member of his team, quarter after quarter, the manager's justification was that he was not convinced to nominate anyone of his team member for any award as he himself was not hitting his target and earning his incentive. Typical "I am not ok; you should also be not ok" syndrome.

Manager's dilemma:

Most manager's face this dilemma of being ethical as well as pragmatic. Few managers think rewarding subordinates for getting things done is manipulative of subordinate's behaviour just like punishing with a view to disciplining for doing something unacceptable.

Just as any amount of reprimanding cannot correct a wrong behaviour, rewards just do not change employee behaviour forever. These are the two methods deployed typically by most managers for manipulating subordinates with the intent to change their behaviour.

The next dilemma is about a choice of team members. Should a manager gather a team of people who just follow the instructions and reward them for the same?

This approach may enable managers in creating a workplace culture in which people feel gagged in the long run, which is not an environment that is conducive to nurturing curiosity, exploration and learning.

Organizations fostering such culture, must expect employees to be constantly working towards winning the confidence of manager through the award. Gaining manager's favoured or for avoiding the manager's ire and reprisal becomes the driver.

Through rewards, the workplace culture that gets created is one where people feel choked and controlled and such environment is not conducive to the free flow of ideas, continuous learning, and progress.

Quite often the top management raises the question about the logic behind additional rewards. The question raised is, "why employees should have any expectation of additional rewards when they get paid for doing their job".

Do employees get motivated enough by getting paid the compensation alone or there is a need to have rewards for specific things to be done? Many would argue that paying people fairly should be enough to motivate to get the job done.

The fact is, in workplaces, employees are not excited by being the receiver of a fair economic value but they are hungry for recognition.

No one wants to stay longer with the organization where their above and beyond work contributions are ignored or go unrecognized, just as the girl who dates won't tolerate the relationship if there is no eye contact in conversations.

What then is fair compensation? In America, even leading companies like Starbucks, Walmart, and McDonalds have faced criticism for paying unfairly even when the company is making a hefty profit.

Income disparities have become highly pronounced, especially in affluent economies. America's top ten- per cent earns nearly nine times as much of the bottom ninety per cent.

The top one per cent of the American managers earns an average pay over thirty-eight times than the bottom ninety-nine per cent. The top-level American executives earn over one hundred eighty-four times the income of the bottom level.

The richest America can boast of one out of every fourteen living below poverty. While the workers' compensation remained static for many years, the executive remuneration has been skyrocketing. The American employers seem to subscribe to the old adage of throwing peanuts to get monkeys

Therefore, the answer to the fair compensation lies in knowing that money is not the primary driver for all employees. Many employees are better motivated and value long time- off, flexible working, work-life balance, and wellness benefits.

In one of the leading Indian IT companies the annual practice is to spend few million rupees for the social meet of all employees by gathering in an exotic five-star resort.

Everyone from the CEO to the office boy travelled to dream location for three nights and four days and the whole company was shut down for this. Everyone travelled by train together and few employees were allowed to bring wife and children.

This is an HR driven event and this just had the effect of proving the point about the value of equality.

Needless to say, people cherished the memories and would not leave the company easily, even if the competitor offered compensation far above.

Dr. Deming wrote in his book "Out of the Crisis" about merit ratings and the rewards attached to them. Many companies have the annual appraisal systems by which everyone receives from his superior a rating.

Then the HR department indulges in moderation of the ratings and slotting people into different levels of performance groups. Management by objectives led to the same evil of Management by the numbers or "Management by fear".

In armed forces and in many of the government-owned organizations, even today the CVR -Confidential reporting-on subordinate's performance is widely adopted. The managers typically use this as a tool to reward or punish subordinates to buy compliance.

There is no feedback given about the performance deficiencies even when the boss resorts to extreme ratings. Obviously, the system is designed to choke any improvement initiative on anything.

In such climate, the pay raise is perceived by employees as an annual ritual and not an event to look forward to by anyone in the armed forces, including the best performers who get the highest raise.

In one study, when employees were asked, the manager's peers ranked pay as number one item while the subordinates ranked pay as the fifth item of importance.

This is a clear manifestation of perception gap which is reflected in the manager's decision-making, when it comes to employee reward or recognition.

The first victim is the interpersonal relationship in an environment of appraisal-based pay raises. Arguments have been made against performance appraisal systems. Pay hikes linked to manager's ratings still is the practice that is widespread.

Moreover, there have been numerous active campaigners against the performance appraisal system in TQM environment. While the performance appraisal focuses on individual, TQM focuses on organizational goals combined with team effort,

Appraisal based rewards end up encouraging competition along with intense rivalry therefore collaboration which is fundamental needed for TQM suffers

Pay hikes linked to appraisal inhibit employees from cooperating with each other as there is compulsion to race against each other.

In any annual performance appraisal process, the forced distribution of ratings leads only to overall discontent.

Soon after completion of the appraisal exercise the HR departments are busy in companies force rank to fit the rating distribution to bell curve.

The pay raises of top percentage are minimized to a few in the top five per cent of the population resulting in disappointment for the majority.

If maximum publicity is given to the award recipient through bulletin boards or newsletters. Distance and divide are created though countless people may sulk without speaking openly about dissatisfaction.

Creating innumerable awards to address every single goal along with wide coverage of the population is impractical. One can only have as many rewards as the budget permits.

Having too few awards can only invite criticism of favouritism or even deliberate fixing by manager to rotate the rewards to minimize dissatisfaction among team members.

When employees are compelled to compete for a few rewards, they are likely to treat even friends as impediments to their own success. The same end result can be achieved without offering rewards which hurt sentiments.

Introducing competition among employees if not handled carefully ends up vitiating the working environment.

If team members' motivations are already low and collaborative work is not the major requirement initiating a bit of competition between teams may work.

When everyone wants leader board as the main plank for motivation, definite strategies that foster healthy competition produces results. In an atmosphere where people are feeling diffident and nurse self-doubt, injecting a competition can work as the real catalyst to drive creative accomplishment and innovation.

The downside of injected competition in certain work environments with greater flexibility pushes people to engage in questionable behaviour and that is something that can be counterproductive. Intense competition can incite unethical behaviour also. It happens frequently with investment bankers when they are given unlimited discretionary powers to trade the way they want with millions of dollars and they are tempted with large incentives as a reward. They end up using their own freedom of choice to take high-risks or to engage in questionable acts. Barings Bank's Nick Leeson is one such example along with another example of inappropriate behaviour by rogue executives of Lehman brothers where intense competition fanned by the temptation of unlimited reward drove people towards unethical behaviour that were promoted by competition.

The average pay and benefits across Lehman's 28,600 employees were $331,958 while the average pay for the top fifty people was about USA $14m. This amounted to the pay of 677 employees. This is a highly disproportionate distribution of compensation.

Some pundits would argue that it is healthy to encourage competition to draw out the best.

This may not be true when group and team thinking and working is required.

Many reasons can be attributed to an employee contributing at lower than expected level. It could be due to lack of cooperation, acts of confrontation from team members or micro-management by the boss.

Under these conditions, introducing the element of severe competition to fuel superior performance through rewards may not work. The conflict or dilemma that arises also is about short-term personal interest vs. long -term goals.

Incentives to boost sales of one brand in one-quarter may be at the cost of a premium brand which the company wants to build over a long period.

Aggressive incentive plans increase the anxiety and vitiate style of the manager to be intimidating and over-anxious. The reward plans alone are not going to solve the performance or motivational issues. Those managers who recommend the reward (the person with authority to nominate and have a say in the decision), ignores the right reasons for which the award was instituted. Having made up the mind the manager tries to justify the selection and build own reasons, making it difficult for the selection committee to decide.

Rewards create dysfunctional leadership. Managers are often tempted to use a reward system as an easy alternative for verbal praise or recognition, positive feedback, emotional and social support, and autonomy on the job.

Accordingly, rewards create a weak and docile leadership style. Manager's effort in tempting subordinates with the incentive as bait for getting the results requires lesser effort than the effort for training, mentoring and educating. There is a better option of challenging and rewarding people with self-confidence.

A professor stood before his class of senior nuclear physics students, about to pass out the final exam. In his address he said "I have been privileged to be your teacher and I know how solid you have all worked to prepare for this final test.

I also know that you are off to higher education next fall. I am well aware of the pressure you are under to keep your GPA up,
I know you are all capable of understanding what is in store in this test material, I am prepared to offer an automatic 'B' to anyone who would prefer not to take the final test".

The relief was visible in the faces of a majority of the students and a number of students jumped up to appreciate the professor and departed from class. The class was left with a handful of students and the offer was repeated giving one last chance.

Only one student decided to leave the class, leaving seven back. The professor closed the door and took roll call and he handed out the envelope containing the final test paper. When the students opened the envelope, they were looking at two sentences typed on a paper "Congratulations, you have just received an 'A' in this class. Keep believing in yourself." The moral is "believers are achievers."

The responsibility is on the manager to find the believers and enlist in the team and encourage them.

Many managers resort to easier option of tempting people with rewards to achieve their own goals, that only helps in staying static in own leadership talent growth.

Organizations that foster pay for performance strategy tend to use fewer creative methods in deploying newer and alternate strategies.

Rewards culture creates ineffective leadership and ill-prepared managers for crisis management during difficult times when rewards disappear.

In one of the recent studies, it was noted that supervisors tended to follow the path of least-efforts or meek leadership style or style of soft task orientation to reach the goals when incentive plans were in place to lean on.

In order to motivate the employees to participate in any activity, organizations have tried various forms of incentive and it has been established that there has not been any better employee involvement. Thus, Rewards blunt the management or leadership abilities which are harmful to the organization.

Some experts observe that pay for performance actually impedes the effectiveness of managers and creates ineffective leadership.

Creativity is the first victim as rewards discourage risk-taking. When an employee gets paid a large incentive for achieving sales the salesman goes to any extent to get the numbers and meet targets. In one extreme level of reaction to aggressive incentive plan a colleague in sales said "I would even sell my mother to earn this kind of money".

Monroe J. Haegele a pay for performance expert is of the view that people will do what they are paid for .When inducement is created to focus on what one has done to get rewarded or merely for doing a task, people are less inclined to think beyond the task and explore newer and superior options.

When enticement is created to focus on what one can do to get rewarded merely for doing a task, people are less inclined to think beyond the task and explore superior and enhanced options. Creative approach is the first fatality of a culture where everyone is made to work for rewards.

Does offering large rewards for simple mechanical skills would produce superior performance?

Does culture influence the impact of rewards?

These two hypotheses were tested in an experiment where a group of students was set up to play a few games, which involved creativity, and motor skills, and concentration. A promise was made on reward for each type. In return for their performance, three levels of - small, medium, and large- rewards were promised.

The task involving only mechanical skills, attracted rewards as one could expect. The rule also promised a higher reward for superior and better performance.

The result of the experiment was that the task which required routine cognitive skill that was tagged with a bigger reward resulted in led to a poorer performance.

Then the test was conducted to see if there was any cultural bias and the researchers went to a small town in India, where the standard of living was much lower compared to many American villages.

In the Indian village, even a modest reward was valued as more meaningful. The participants were offered the same set of games, and same three levels of rewards.

The performance of the people who were working towards a medium or higher level of rewards was not very significantly better or higher than those who worked for lower levels of rewards.

The people who were offered the highest rewards, performed at inferior level in eight of the nine tasks proving the point that promise of higher incentives may not induce superlative performance.

The late professor of Cornell University, John Condry, had opined that rewards are the enemies of exploration. The first victim of reward culture is innovation. A company's sales analysis indicated that they were only getting marginal revenue growth and that too was from existing customers, and the sales directors hardly were signing up any new customers.

The CEO realized that the company managed to survive because of high retention of old customers and someday they would face stunted growth he came up with an idea to change the sales incentive plan with a substantial portion of the weighting for booking orders from new platinum (annual order potential over million dollars) accounts. The baseline goal was as three accounts per quarter. The reward was huge cash incentive.

After experimenting for two- quarters, the incentive scheme had to be scrapped because everyone neglected the existing accounts and put efforts without success on new accounts resulting in a sharp fall in the total billing.

The Rewards can undermine espoused company values of quality or market excellence. There is no other driving force that can match the power of those values.

People who do exceptional work are generally receptive to the idea to get compensated better in basic wages and even be gladder when they feel non- discriminated and fairly paid.

Psychology of high performing employees is that they do not work to collect a pay-check or incentives. They work because of their inherent passion for excellence in what they do.

With extrinsic motivation, one may not focus on the job and may be tempted to procrastinate. Getting the reward at the end is the singular goal, but one may not care much about being perfect or excellent. If the reward is absent, there is no inherent urge to work. External motivational systems are easier to design and inject than the intrinsic motivation.

Rewards, like discipline, have the tendency to actually damage the intrinsic driving force that is essential for bringing out a higher level of performance.

When managers place more stress on high the earning potential for higher performance at work, it turns out that subordinates exhibit less interest in the work itself and they perceive it as bait with some ulterior motives.

The Contingent payment system has an adverse effect on the intrinsic motivation. Offering huge rewards for complicated tasks does not really end up encouraging the expected behaviour, but the effect is counterproductive or even destructive. It is worthwhile to be aware as to where the motivation originates.

It starts in our brain where a neurotransmitter, called dopamine puts the spark of a chemical message to alert us on the task.

The message is spread by the interaction with various receptors. This process gets more complicated when the transmission is multiplied throughout the entire brain.

The pathway dopamine takes decides the level of motivation. The dopamine-pleasure linkage has been validated by many different studies.

The impact of Dopamine's on our body is in many different areas, including motivation. It affects memory, behaviour and cognition, learning and pleasurable reward. When a reward is aimed at specific behaviour, it tends to send a certain message to the recipient about what was done and manipulates the future behaviour. When a large segment of the employees feels controlled or manipulated through rewards, the tendency of disinterest creeps in what people are being told to do.

A glass laboratory ware manufacturing factory had faced continuously, low production problem. While negotiating the union contract the management had offered an unexpected level of incentive for getting a better level of finished products but it involved a bit complicated, but an improved way of packing which would have ensured minimum breakage. The union immediately suspected that they were being even tricked by the management.

The behaviour of urgency addiction to complete the work is not self-directed, but it is the reward that drives the behaviour.

Rewards decrease intrinsic motivation which is the concern behind the psychology of rewards.

People work with a feeling of suspicion and think that managers have hidden agenda. Rewards thus undermine espoused company values.

Researchers have confirmed the hypotheses

That, "Larger the incentive, higher is the negativity". It appeared that large rewards in fact undermine and kill the integrity, enthusiasm and the passion for the job.

Whenever there is a promise of huge incentive or pay hike for temporary goal-oriented performance the system merely makes the employees be less enthusiastic about the job on hand and people tend to approach the task with a lower degree of commitment to excellence.

Rewards have an important role to play compelling to push people forward, but the human dynamism is more complex to address with money as bait. Companies aiming to get lasting effect must cultivate a culture of opportunities for personal excellence and visionary approach. Company culture plays a crucial role in employee attitude.

How does that happen?

Five monkeys were put in a cage with swings, tyres, toys to play and have fun. As bait few bananas were hung from a hook at the top of a ladder. Seeing the banana, one of the bold ones climbs up the ladder and goes for the bananas, and suddenly a bucket of cold-water shower falls on the monkey. This completely rattles the monkey and it scrambles down immediately.

After some time, the second monkey now decided to try the luck to get the banana. It also gets the bucket of cold shower and all the monkeys, one by one meet with the same fate of cold-shower. Soon the monkey brigade gives up trying and all of them huddle in one corner while the bananas were rotting.

One of the monkeys in the cage was replaced with a new monkey and the new monkey with full energy goes for the bananas. This time no cold shower was applied, but before the monkey could reach the bananas, the old monkeys start beating up the new monkey and pull him down.

Very quickly he gives up the attempt and climbs down and settles with the older monkeys in the corner; second monkey now was replaced the new monkey also goes for the bananas.

Soon all the monkeys, including the replaced one attack the newer one. All monkeys were replaced one after another.

Every time a monkey attempted to grab the bananas; he was attacked by all the other monkeys – even though none of the monkeys had actually faced the cold shower. We often hear the remarks from older employees that "things happen here in this way only". This is very typical of the organization culture.

The older employees, who are used to a typical established way of doing things, resist change and any attempt by newer employees also gets pulled down. Attempting cultural changes is always a difficult and time-consuming process. This the toughest challenge for leadership. Meek attempt to change employee behaviour through incentives may not work.

Employee engagement and retention is directly related to the extent of care and concern that management shows in employee's competency enhancement and career progression.

Maintaining the satisfaction level is not sufficient to retaining people and make them highly productive. Engaged employees are more open and have positive feelings about the company and radiate that emotion while communicating with others.

Engaged employees are positive and value the encouragement they get towards success in their job. Engaged employees do not carry the resignation letter in their pocket and boast about better offers in peer conversations. Thus, the engaged employees are more productive than the satisfied employees.

4. The Variable pay Myth and Magic.

In this chapter, the important issues of variable pay and linkage of the incentive payments to the performance targets are discussed. The disproportionate pay for top management executives and its linkage to unethical behaviour is also explored.

If the answer to the following questions is affirmative, the probability of any incentive scheme achieving the expected results is very high.

- The employees have been given specific goals by the manager and the current level of performance on those goals is lower than the targets?
- The reason for low performance is lack of motivation and not the lack of skill.
- Appropriate and stable mechanism to measure current and desired performance is in place?
- The goals must be challenging, but reasonable and realistic.

Especially before setting up huge incentive plans based on performance, one must examine if similar plans had delivered results. in fact, there is strong evidence to point out that the hefty variable incentives are counterproductive and encourage executives to manipulate the metrics.

Studies have shown that when senior executives, including the CEO, were paid huge stock options, the probability of them manipulating revenue figures increased. The globe sized recent scams in Enron, Wells Fargo, and Lehman have reinforced the general belief that the efficiency of control mechanisms in financial markets and regulatory reforms anywhere in the world including the USA is far from adequate.

In developed economies as well as in most primitive type economies the corporate governance fails to check earnings manipulation by people in leadership.

Even companies like Xerox, had the reputation of manipulations of revenue to the tune of 1.5 billion dollars. This unethical behaviour only resulted in shareholder lawsuits and product safety problems. Same is the case with performance incentives which encourage executives to indulge in the high-risk behaviour and they resort to working on short-term strategies for personal gains.

The objective and principle of any employee rewards must be to encourage ethical and the appropriate behaviour. Hence, the C level executives must have only fixed compensation to keep them away from temptation.

They must have the benefit of an adequate return on their investment, similar to other shareholders. Similarly, there is no logic behind exorbitant base pay for the CEOs consisting of base salaries and hefty a variable amount based on profit criteria.

If running a business is a teamwork and collective effort, rewarding few at the top with disproportionate compensation does create the divide among the employees.

There is enough evidence to show that incentive pay is effective for routine tasks and top executives' do not have routine tasks.

When people are working on creative tasks with a mandate to produce innovative solutions, offering a major portion of the pay as variable ends up merely hurting performance.

The classic example is that of a challenge thrown at Air Force pilots to land a certain number of planes in a given time, and they were offered high incentives.

The offer of hefty incentive did not produce the desired results, but the performance of the pilots considerably deteriorated. This was because of the tasks requiring learning.

There is a famous saying which says "if you want exemplary performance, then it is the wrong goal to fixate on".

Several studies have shown that when tasks involved learning, developing new competencies, managing newer situations, paying hefty incentives rarely produced the expected results.

In fact, various studies over the last twenty years, especially the studies by Kanfer and Ackerman, as well as Kanfer and Edwin Locke, have established that, in work situations where learning is important, the carrot of incentive pay did not work.

When employees are driven by an inner urge and motivated, they do things for self-satisfaction and a sense of achievement. When employees are extrinsically motivated, they do things because of the rewards they hope to receive.

When a company structures remuneration for senior managers, topping it with substantial variable pay as the incentive, hoping that it will drive performance, in many occasions, the temptation is only for finding dishonest ways to earn that incentive.

An IT company in Ohio, USA had established a sizable market and revenue to the tune of twenty million dollars in a very niche area of government departments with a data analytic IT solution. In two years, the company attracted the proposal for takeover. Finally, the merger took place with another BI boutique company. The due diligence was not done enough to check the invoicing methods. The sales figures were inflated and shown to be growing by leaps and bounds for government sector clients.

The maverick CEO bargained to be retained to run the show on the same compensation level. After two years of the acquisition, it was found out by the CFO that the accounting practice adopted by the CEO was flawed.

He had allowed booking the total contract value of the IT contract as a sale and drawing his sales incentive every quarter. The contract included milestone delivery related invoicing and 180 days credit for payment.

This means the company booked a virtual sale while the CEO had cashed out his incentive. The company that acquired ended up with the dud sales and incurred a big loss.

The data of the compensation received in 2006 by a few of the employees who pushed the employer companies into a gigantic mess and a massive loss for the State and shareholders.

Bear Stearns CEO, James Cayne, was paid thirty- four million dollars, and he delivered a death blow to Bear Stearns besides costing two and a half-billion dollars to the taxpayer.

Lehman Brothers had the CEO in Richard Fuld, and he took home twenty-seven million dollars as the salary. He delivered the biggest financial crisis worldwide and the recession of 2007-08.

Charles Prince was the CEO of Citigroup and got paid $25 million and his deliberate actions brought the Citi's stock price down from $50 a share to $3.50 which made innocent investors lose heavily.

Countrywide Financial paid forty-three million dollars for the CEO Angelo Mozilo. A single person could demolish the complex subprime market completely robbing millions of common people.

The senior executives of Wells Fargo, who were rewarded with massive bonuses, resorted to charging thousands of uninformed customers exorbitant foreign transaction fees, recently. The fee charged was the highest foreign transaction fee, which was set at eight times higher than industry standards.

It is the aggressive incentive plan which triggered the temptation and drove the executives to indulge in unethical behaviour.

A bank which is the custodian of public money was happy to pay one hundred eighty-five million dollars for "widespread illegal" sales practices and bury the issue. No executive thought the act of directing and pressuring

Lower-level bank employees to open accounts without customers' knowledge, as unethical because the lure of huge reward was overwhelming.

The motive can only be attributed to the temptations and greed to earn windfall incentive in the shortest possible time.

5. Strategies, Design and the Policies.

It said that things are created not once but twice. The mental creation is the first and then the physical creation. Thus, engineering an effective reward, recognition plan, policies and strategies require a deep and thorough understanding of the organization's priorities, culture as well as the competencies of the managers. This chapter will cover some of those design ideas.

Key issues involved in employee reward plans are about the design, the process, the administration, the internal marketing and the communication. The goals are the same for every management. To achieve peak level performance through motivating employees, retaining them and make them highly engaged.

The first principle is that the employee reward plans have to be based on corporate philosophies on people management. The bias for action comes only if there is a strong principle to back action.

Then only the HR department gets the legitimacy to establish practices, structures and procedures to design and constantly assess appropriate types and levels of rewards, benefits and other forms of recognition. The next best requirement is to continuously monitor the competitive environment.

It is absolutely necessary to stay competitive as reward management is not just giving some benefit. Issues are also linked with those non-financial rewards which cater to intrinsic or extrinsic motivation.

The twelve key issues that will help designing sound reward plans:

- Support to the organization's business priorities. (Innovation, customer service, quality, market leadership etc.).
- Type of employee needs being satisfied (security, stability or career development).
- Maintaining internal equity. Not paying attention to equity can create a feeling of unfairness which leads to low morale and low productivity leading to low engagement.
- Individual performance and contribution or promoting teamwork.
- The Robust performance assessment process is the key to objective reward for individual performance
- The manager's skill to assess and administer the reward process.
- Rewarding high achievers while not demoralizing the average performers.
- Managing reward processes consistently without bending the rules of the game and still being flexible.

- The motivation for those who stagnate at the top of the pay band.
- Delivering the communication properly and consistently.
- Checks and balances for not creating windfall situations.
- Balancing the budget.
- Maintaining competitiveness in the marketplace.

- What is trending in the reward scene in India? The attitude of managements towards a fair and adequate reward has undergone changes in recent years, driven by the demands of the new younger generation of the workforce. Employees tend to value more the recognition with fairness, frequency and the sense of appreciation.

The annual increment rituals are no longer eagerly awaited event as an attraction by the employees and that event seems to only trigger more attrition after the pay raise announcement. The reason for the post-increment attrition is that, many organizations do not have proper performance assessment tools or systems combined with skilful managers who can handle the performance appraisal process and the feedback. They do not have any scientifically collected compensation data to fall back on pay decisions.

The age-old tradition of "Festival bonus' in India has also become a disappointment in terms of inducing loyalty. Festival bonus has transformed to be an entitlement. Indian employees seem to prefer a bigger bonus than a 10 to 12 % annual raise.

Information Technology companies, though fewer, in initiating the creative ways of rewarding, seem to set new normal. Recent reward offerings vary from Mercedes cars to iPhones and paid international vacations.

These high-cost rewards are becoming popular (especially in India) and are being deployed to attract younger talents. Privately owned companies are rewarding employees with cars and family apartments, radiating the message of work hard, and get rewarded. As health issues matter, companies are learning to address employees' and family health through annual health checks, and group medical insurance.

Most managements desire to create a rewards program "to keep up with the Joneses". Any formal or informal reward, recognition plan should keep in mind that there is more power in the act of acknowledging an employee's smallest and simplest contribution or accomplishment than giving a huge monetary reward.

Genuine appreciation touches the emotional chord if done sincerely. That is the power of simple recognition just as the Ubuntu. It is not to suggest that one should do away with any form of monetary rewards.

I worked as Plant HR manager in a manufacturing setup that made laboratory ware.

The plant worked all three shifts and being a continuous process plant, it worked round the clock throughout the year. The glassblower or forming crew employee was recruited only if the person was related to one another in some way. The mouth blowing required the crew to blow turn by turn to blow the molten glass to the shape of huge flask.

The skill could be learned only on the job by spending years under a master blower. The working conditions on the shop floor were severe and most hazardous with fire, heat and dust all around

The fire hazard was very high due to the use of oxygen and LPG. The glass melting furnace and fire lathes need highly inflammable oxygen and other combustible items. Everyone works on fire lathe or works near the furnace.

Workers need to drink bottles of barley water frequently to avoid dehydration as the temperature inside the plant and especially near the furnace was 1400 to 1600 degree centigrade.

That is the temperature at which silica melts to produce glass. Imagine trying motivation tricks in such conditions to get more output.

The workers belonged to multiple unions and besides heat; the work atmosphere was always tense. Productivity was obviously below the standard and low. Management tried production incentive plans to get more production.

Being a newcomer, I thought it was easier to solve the problem if only the plant shift supervisors changed their attitude towards their crew. The issue was heavy breakage and loss.

Targeting my attention to reduce the wastage, I talked informally to the workers. I found out there were simple ways to reduce the breakage by over seventy per cent. Taking the initiative, I made the supervisors to tell their crew members, especially those who worked on night shift that the crew members will be chosen for recognition if they get more finished items into the pack.

At the end of each shift, the crew member who packed more would win a badge from the crew captain and would be presented the badge on the shop floor in front of all other workers. (Peer to peer).

With ten such badges the employee becomes an "employee of the year" and similar public recognition was done on the shop floor in front of all workers during the day shift. Needless to say, that there was almost sixty per cent increase in the quantity of manufactured wares that went to pack.

Inter-union competition was forgotten. Supervisors' apathy vanished. Pride in work was victorious. What monetary incentive could not achieve a simple recognition could achieve.

Our brain has over hundred billion neurons and every one of them is connected to thousands of other neurons. If there is one thing in this world that is yet to be conquered it is the human brain. An estimate indicates that with even the latest technology, it would take thirty years with the deployment of ten thousand automated microscopes to map the connections between every neuron in a human brain, and a hundred million terabytes of storage space. Such is the complexity. It is the power horse, the seat of intelligence, and controller of behaviour.

Very few managers are aware that feeling good has the biological reason and the Oxytocin is responsible for that feeling. Known as "love hormone" oxytocin is created in the brain by pituitary glands when one feels loved or appreciated.

This is why recognition assumes importance. A good hug or handshake generates Oxytocin and has an impact on individual's social behaviour and emotional responses.

Employees can be helped at no cost to achieve the psychological stability. Whenever Oxytocin is generated people in work settings are motivated to perform better and feel most trustworthy. In the semi-annual "2011 Workforce Mood Tracker™ Report" by Globo force, who specializes in employee appreciation, 39 per cent of employees reported feeling unappreciated at work, and more than half were dissatisfied with the level of appreciation shown.

Giving a praise or appreciation to even own team members or direct reports or any other colleague at workplaces for a job well done is a very difficult act for many managers. The act does not come spontaneously and very naturally though it works totally in the manager's favour.

Most of the employees believe that timely recognition would reduce voluntary turnover. The Majority of the employees who do not feel properly acknowledged and recognized would not go beyond defined job descriptions or formal rules.

The biggest motivator for any subordinate is the timely appreciation, radiating genuine feelings combined with proper body language. The act of recognition must radiate the genuine feeling and has to be consistent. The recognition cannot be a tool for favouritism.

It has to be timely and instant in execution.

The Essential rules:

Avoid reward being given at frequent interval. Try and give the award every day or week only to find that the awards become a joke in the organization. Even if, it is a mere pat on the back certificate better to make it fortnightly and make it feel good for the person to earn it.

Not given more than once to the same person for defined interval. There is no fun in proving a point that someone in your team is a star.

If the same person is awarded repeatedly it not only creates heartbreak for others, but works against the individual by creating an image of the most favoured.

Avoid making the reward once in a blue moon event after a long interval. Longer the gap, the effectiveness and thrill are lost. No one will look forward to getting the reward and would not even try.

Avoid making it "as and when you like to do". There has to be certainty of time for people expecting to work towards the reward. The danger of not laying down a process and not communicating it well in advance is it makes the reward plan to be an off-the-cuff decision and very unpredictable.

Do not lay down too many goals and conditions. Make it appropriate and relevant to the driver and specific to one single objective.

Do not link eligibility to the length of time spent in the organization in order to even qualify for the reward.

Even if you wish to define a minimum time of six months period would be good enough to avoid any embarrassment if the employee decides to quit for any reason.

In influencing the effects of reinforcement, the neural structures play a critical role. A reward acts like a stimulator.

A reward is a handy tool for altering behaviour as rewards serve as the reinforcers. A reinforcer is something that enhances the probability of the behaviour to reoccur when introduced immediately after the behaviour. Just by naming something as a reward, one does not expect to produce the reinforcer effect. A reward acts as a reinforcer only if it increases the probability of a repeat behaviour. Reward or reinforcement is perceived by the recipient to be delivering the positive value. Recognition is the best reinforcer of the desired behaviour, practices,

principle-based conduct, and values.

It is the managers' skill and attitude to deploy recognition for being effective and successful. Through recognition, managers can promote trust and respect and it facilitates and encourages change. Timely recognition drives improvement and creates a positive work environment. Above all, it improves the quality of work life as there is genuine trust.

Recognition motivates individuals and teams to do their best and enhances loyalty as it addresses the basic human need to feel acknowledged and appreciated. Recognition reflects commitment to each other and inspires accomplishment and achievement.

Giving praise often makes people feel good. When there is a positive feedback from a manager or anyone from the leadership role about an employee's output at work-place, that psychological stroke has the potential to enhance that employee's self-esteem and pride tremendously.

The transmission of information from one neuron to the next is done by dopamine. The release of dopamine a neurotransmitter helps to control the pleasure centres of the brain. In addition to generating good feeling, dopamine also triggers innovative thinking and creative problem-solving at work, opine many experts.

When we generate the good feeling through recognition, we enhance the skills of people. The effective way to have an enduring impact on employee engagement, is giving positive feedback regularly.

The effects of tangible rewards on employees can be counterproductive. When experimented with children and adults the promise of reward actually reduced the desire. The negative effect on intrinsic motivation was established in the research experiment. Tangible rewards given even for good performance typically decreased the inner force for activities which the people love to do.

Children who were fond of drawing were not that driven to do better. when they were told about an exciting reward compared to the control group of children who were told of reward after they finished their work.

Monetary rewards have even been found to choke creativity and problem-solving.

The social psychology behind workplace is that employees are made to bond and every human treats the experience at the workplace as an opportunity to bond.

This makes public recognition even more powerful. Just as the body needs food for nourishment, the psychological or psycho-spiritual nourishment can come from the celebrations. We humans are fond of celebrating achievements and building stories about accomplishments and love to share the moment with colleagues, which generate joy and happy feeling.

Sam Walton, the founder of Wal-Mart reportedly used to visit the stores incognito and place one dollar note in the staff room refrigerator.

After his round in the store, whoever in the store was engaging in customer wow, got that autographed one dollar note, in the stand-up meeting?

Sam would call out loudly the name and reveal his identity while announcing the name. That was a "moment of truth for the employee and it created memorable experience.

The psychology behind human nature is to gather things that are considered very valuable and show off, especially when someone attains fame and status. That is the reason for the plaques with years of service inscribed on it is appealing to those who value the recognition and social status that follows. The intense desire to acquire and collect material possessions can be exploited to motivate people.

As human beings, we all have the instinct and are biologically motivated to defend our possessions. Roger Federer or Raphael Nadal is not letting go their world number one rank or top seed in grand slam without a fight. Number one salesman never easily would let go that ranking.

The employee engagement driven and supported by strong recognition programs will enable people to put their best effort and protect their organizations against competitive threats.

Decision- making becomes difficult for most of the managements in making a choice between cash or non-cash rewards and the proportion.

The real image is accessed from the right brain. Symbolism is enduring in mind. Therefore, a balanced mix of both cash and non-cash is likely to be accepted.

Cash Rewards.

Recently MIT scientists reported about where and how abstract ideas are stored in the human brain. The concept of cash is an abstraction and that does not leave lasting image. The brain stores abstraction in the left, logical side. This is accessed less frequently in less detail. Therefore, the memories of cash rewards are short-lived and forgotten quickly.

While designing reward programs, it is better to go for simple plans which are proliferated widely and send a strong signal of care and concern. If an employee has to wait it out for the whole year to win an award, lesser is the chance that the employee will work for it or even if he wins the award fails to get the message and make a positive behavioural change.

The power of value-driven culture cannot just be ignored. Behaviour modifications linked to corporate values create intense engagement.

Peer recognition

Traditionally it was always the boss who had the privilege to praise or reward the subordinate. Instead, when the peer to peer recognition is done it turns out to be the most powerful and it creates "culture of mutual respect". Employees in same level in the hierarchy rarely give each other open praise or rewards and when they do, it makes a huge emotional impact.

When employees are given rewards instantly from any peer even by way of a "Thank you" card, which works as a magic in bonding.

It is not the nature of the work or workplace that is generating fun at work-place but the gesture of peer recognition can.

How to Create the Moments of Magic for the Employee.

One can create numerous reward schemes, but the execution makes all the difference. It is how one creates "moment of magic" that wins the heart of those winning the award.

The award announcement has to create the tempo and make the event memorable.

One strategy I had adopted, was to hand over the winning trophy or the check at the hands of his immediate boss. The possibility was that not all of them happened to be good at making speech or making presentation. Hence, the HR department works overtime to prepare them to speak in front of an audience.

The script is written and handed over to the supervisor and rehearsed thoroughly. The Suspense is maintained throughout the presentation and name is revealed at the end. The build-up is made with the supervisor narrating the small anecdotes about the winner.

His likings, hobbies were recalled and the supervisor speaks about the reasons for the award. The employee is given the photograph of the event along with the certificate for chosen for the award.

This process achieves many things.

This event creates the magic. Second in the eyes of the employees the image of the supervisor goes up which goes a long way to maintain camaraderie.

Sam Walton was known to create the "moments of magic" for the employees. He would always be visiting Wal-Mart stores to check for himself how the employees live in the true spirit of Walmart. One day during a store visit he found a new associate struggling to fold clothes for display. Sam offered to help and sought the permission to teach her a better way. He spent the next few hours in showing her the proper way to do the job.

Many managers would have handled this in a very ordinary way. The normal tendency of any supervisor is to point out her mistakes and few supervisors would have even rebuked her for wasting the time. A true leader he was and Sam Walton would do none of that. He would identify and praise anyone for their good aspects of trying hard.

Secondly, Sam didn't take credit for making her a better employee, but considered it as his duty to elevate the performance of a new employee.

He chose to recognize the employee's effort and always encouraged learning. Walton always gave public recognition for people who are eager learners just as he did in this case.

The anecdote leaves few takeaways.

Recognition must be authentic if the employee behaviour is worth recognizing. What then is being authentic? Managers at times use the rewards to please their team members or those who are favourites. In one case the manager even used to tell everyone in the team that they would get the reward by rotation.

These are not being authentic and the reward loses its purpose of reinforcing desired behaviour. It is not always the result, but sometimes the effort needs praise.

On the spot" awards from peers when working even in different teams go a long way besides empowering and becoming the powerful factor behind employee engagement.

Despite all these rewards, employees feel engaged if they own a part of the organization. Does ESOP play the role in employee engagement or loyalty? Next chapter goes into detail

6. The Employee Stock Option Plans

In this chapter, we explore whether the strategy to retain employees through the reward of an Employee Stock Option plan will work. The impact of ESOP on the motivation of employees to perform better is also examined. Is the ESOP the modern-day invention of the reward for loyalty? Questions about different variations of Stock options are

deliberated in this chapter.

Every startup company, apart from raising the money, is facing the question of attracting the critical and key talents to form the team, which will share the founders' vision and passion without burning the scarce cash. Stock options have provided a platform and the opportunity to share success directly. The size of the company, the cost of administration, continuous support of the ESOP, can be the prime factors coming in the way before the ESOP offer.

What started as the best business practice primarily for top-level executives is now shifting the focus to cover all permanent payroll employees?
The Board of Directors or the compensation committee authorize the allocation of shares the alternate way some SME adopt is to create a trust fund into which
contributions of new shares of its own stock or cash
to buy existing shares are made. This method could create a market for closely held stock of departing
shareholders.

ESOP through registered Trust:

As per the Indian Trust act, a Trust deed is prepared is registered with
Sub- Registrar. Stocks are then transferred to the Trust from the company.
The required quantity is either through fresh allotment or
by procurement from
existing shareholders in the open market or allocation from the owner of the company.
The Trust can borrow through loans from a bank or financial institution or borrow from the company itself.
The trusts are permitted to borrow money for purchasing the shares.
The shares are allotted on the exercise of their right. Many

technology start-ups and private companies that use ESOPs as their exit strategy. Many companies use ESOPs as a
powerful tool for succession planning.
ESOPs have served as an excellent reward mechanism for the employees and managers who help the company during the initial stages of the struggle. In the USA,
fifty-seven per cent of the total's ESOP issued were from
Manufacturing, professional, technical, scientific services, insurance, finance and
real-estate sector. Information Technology contributed a mere
one per cent.
Forty-five per cent of the plans were created before 1997.
In Japan, over three hundred companies showed enhanced interest by introducing
variations of these ESOP plans, with forty per cent of
them granting shares to
workers. The trend in Japanese companies is moving towards the use of stock grants to motivate employees.
The number of companies giving grants increased by 340% in the last few years.
As per data available, there were 114 large size
European companies from Austria, Switzerland, Denmark, Germany, Spain, Finland, France, Hungary, Ireland, Italy, Netherlander, Norway, Sweden and the UK were contemplating employee share ownership in 2016. The latest edition of the "Barometer of Employee Share Ownership Policies in European Countries" outlined the recent

policy choices in Europe, which showed higher incentives for employee ownership with the exception of France.

A favourable tax approach is being introduced in Poland and Sweden for small and medium sized companies, effective January 2018.

In Ireland Companies can offer shares in multiple ways. Profit-sharing Schemes-Up to a limit, the employer is permitted to give an employee the shares in the company which is tax-free.

Share Options- These Schemes enable employees to save from pay and purchase share options in the employer's company. Mostly these schemes are tax-friendly and effective.

Key Employee Engagement Program (KEEP) is the share-based remuneration to key employees enables small and medium-sized enterprises (SMEs) to maintain their competitiveness and remain effective in the recruitment and retention of key employees. In Ireland, a new share-based incentive mainly for Small and Medium Enterprises was introduced to come into effect in 2018.

Many of these social reformation developments have confirmed the positive trend.

Many European countries have made favourable and tax-friendly policy decisions regarding employee ownership.

France is leading EU nations with the number one spot for employee share ownership in Europe, though in recent years the tax laws have choked the advantage by removing or decreasing fiscal incentives.

The new "Economic Survey of Employee Share Ownership in European Countries", revealed that the stake held by employees in large European companies continues to rise and touched 3.20% in 2016. Even during the economic crisis, employee ownership is the schemes that serve as the engine of participation.

ESOP companies can hope to build a culture of cost-consciousness, innovation, productivity and superior performance.

A study by the Toronto stock exchange revealed that those companies offering ESOP generated better and higher profit growth in a span of a five-year period. The companies which offered ESOP earned ninety-five per cent higher net margins. They also realized better productivity.

Those companies who offered the ESOP posted a ten per cent premium in the stock market, over ninety per cent higher return on the equity, better returns on the capital, and thirty per cent lower debts /equity ratio. In many countries, the government regulations have made ESOPs are complex to install and administer and the cost of establishing and maintaining an ESOP plan can be greater than many other types of retirement plans like 401 k or government-regulated Employee pension plans or even the superannuation plans.

The complexities of tax issues, administrative issues and compliance issues can be tackled only by an expert consultant who has the subject mastery of the legal, as well as accounting aspects.

Starting and administering an ESOP is a tedious and time-consuming project and is not for the weak-hearted managements.

The reason for lack of popularity among non-technology companies may be due to the problem of administrative hurdles.

The History of Employee Stock Option/Employee stock ownership plan dates back to 1956.The very first ESOP idea was born out of the founder's sincere belief that employees who helped in the growth in the initial stages by giving their sweat must become the logical owners of the business. In 1956 Louis O. Kelso, a San Francisco lawyer created the stock ownership plan.

This was to create the ideal solution for succession and transition of Peninsula Newspapers.

Mostly, the information technology start-ups have patronized the ESOP to attract and retain scarce talents. There is a considerable perception gap between what employers see and the employees see. Employers seem to treat ESOP as a reward for retention and the employees perceive this as a legitimate reward for their contribution to the company's growth.

In recent times ESOP has become difficult to administer and complex to comprehend. Compliance norms under the rules for companies about the Share Capital and Debenture are very stringent.

ESOP generally is made available to permanent employees and the whole time and part-time directors.

Another variation is called sweat equity, which has its own set of restrictions.

As per Indian laws, the ESOP can be granted to the founders after being in business for one year and one cannot transfer shares allocated for a minimum period of three years.

The promoter or director holding more than ten per cent stake, are barred from restructuring their own compensation package. There are other similar plans like the restricted stock, stock appreciation rights, phantom stocks, employee equity purchase plans which are used in allotment of shares in lieu of a bonus or incentives for non-cash consideration. The circumstances and facts will be the basis for choosing a scheme

Incentive Stock Option.

Incentive stock options or qualified stock options are granted to employees and this comes with tax benefits.

Some Tax authorities levy lower capital gains tax on ISO and not the regular income tax. ISOs go by the name incentive share options or Qualified Stock Options.

Restricted Stock Units.

Many public technology companies preferred RSO than the traditional stock options for their own advantages. For Restricted stock payment is not usually required it is merely common stock that vests. The restricted stock holder is not allowed to sell the

shares until they vest. The issuing company mostly retains the right to repurchase all unvested shares upon the termination of the holder's employment. In order to attract and retain rare skills, for example, a company might offer one thousand RSU with a face value of ten and with vesting period of five years.

The first year the person gets two hundred, second year three hundred etc. At the five-year period all one thousand is allotted. Unlike Stock RSUs attract tax when they become vested and liquid.

Stock Appreciation Rights:

As indicated by the name The Stock Appreciation Rights fetch the benefit of cash or shares equivalent to the price appreciation of the company's stock over a specified period. SAR motivates everyone work toward the goal of increased stock price which benefit all.

Phantom stock option:

Phantom stock options are made through a contract between a corporation and employees who get the right to encash payment at a designated future time or designated event. The pay-out depends on the actual market value of shares of the corporation. As the price goes up, the pay-out increases.

This is a better way to align the individual's goal with the company's goal.

Not only employees, but directors, or even third-party vendors can be given phantom stocks. Start-up companies have been using phantom stocks as a better performance motivator than ESOP.

\

The normal process is to negotiate in advance the vesting schedules and
pay-out to events like change of management control or any liquidity event.

The flexibility of the agreement and the minimal legal and tax filing paperwork are added advantage Some companies use phantom shares instead of a cash bonus plan.

ESOP for employees in Private Companies in India:

A company which is not listed on the stock exchange is a private company. Private companies are restricted in issuing ESOP for more than fifteen per cent of total paid up equity share capital in a year. The issue value cannot exceed Rupees Fifty million and prior approval of the Central Government is needed.

The Companies Act, 1956 and Unlisted Companies (Issue of Sweat Equity Shares) Rules, 2003 regulate the issuance of sweat equity shares or formulation and implementation of Employee Stock Option Plan or Scheme "ESOP" or "ESOS" by Unlisted Companies (public or private).

Normally Sweat Equity shares are often given as a reward for people who join early and provide technical know-how.

The shares are given at a discounted price or for consideration other than cash.

The Company makes available pre-determined number of shares at a discount.

A company can give options anytime unlike Sweat equity. Numerous amendments to the sections have been made since the introduction. Sweat equity shares normally have lock-in period of three years from the date of allotment.

Fair Market price is assessed and calculated by an independent valuer and the valuation is a key aspect in the unlisted stocks. Sweat equity is given to the founders for non-cash consideration. Typically for providing technical know-how and given after the company has been in business for one year.

As per Indian rules a company cannot issue more than fifteen per cent of its total paid-up capital by way of sweat equity.

Transfer of shares is restricted to a minimum period of three years. Employees allotted can gift to close family members such shares allotted and such gift will not attract Capital Gains Tax. Sweat equity is mainly used for motivating those employees who contributed significantly through technical know-how for consideration other than cash.

The laws and rules applicable- The Companies Act along with the rules of the Security Exchange Board of India.

The Income tax rules are all having implications on ESOP.

Many start-ups in India still issue a letter stating grant of options at the time of recruitment which is not a valid and legal method. Moreover, it leads to disputes and disappointments because of the misunderstandings.

Employment is governed by the contract established in the employment letter. Hence the ESOP scheme must address all the entitlement issues properly during employment, and after termination for all the options granted and vested.

The employment may be terminated for cause or for some reason by giving the agreed notice and the termination may be non-voluntary. The scheme must address the status of options in both cases.

The employee might exercise few of the options and might become a shareholder in the company, and the termination might be an event after the exercise of the option. The employer may not want the person to join the competition. The legal implication of restricting the right for employment must be assessed from legal experts and documented.

Employees must understand the terms and conditions thoroughly to appreciate what they are rewarded how and when they will benefit. There must be clarity about

the option grant, vesting, vesting schedule, when and how to exercise vested options, exercise price etc.

Companies determine the quantum of options based on the level, years of service, and performance.

They decide the weightage for each of these parameters and arrive at the quantum of option grants based on the total points scored.

Many companies place more weightage for staying longer and performing. ESOPs are not a good idea for employees who are risk adverse people.

There are stringent Income tax implications and the cash outflow issues if someone is buying the options.

A great way of rewarding employees who put their heart towards organizational success, is by offering ESOP, but complications made through capital gains tax, income tax etc., have taken away some of the shine.

When Flip kart India approved buyback of $100 million in employee stock options (ESOPs) it was a huge reward for not only its existing employees, but for former employees also.

The tax treatment for employees will differ in the case of unlisted stocks when the buyback happens. In case of buy back, Section forty-six- A of the Income tax act is applicable and Section Sixty-Eight of the Companies Act, 2013 where securities are defined to include stock options also has an impact.

The profit which is the main attraction, received by the employee shall be taxable as capital gains. Stock Options have not really always delivered millions.

The ownership does have an impact to an employee until the employee perceives that ownership of the asset or property is there to lose. The managements have to connect employees to the ownership concept and power it brings.

Most of the technology company employees have been lured by the positive stories about ESOPs and often fail to do their own math and homework to understand the scheme.

The key rules and conditions governing the grants are so rigorous that one cannot get the stocks easily.

Most start-ups which introduce ESOP provide help through HR Department and through one to one session with expert consultants to educate employees explaining how ESOPs work
and how employees benefit.
In India, though initially, ESOPs were novel idea and attractive.

Various tax measures, regulations and restrictions brought in by company law regulators have taken the shine away. Many IT companies started issuing the ESOP followed by manufacturing companies; infrastructure and even public sector companies started offering ESOP.

Globally the ESOPs are heavily regulated in every country and keeping in tune with regulatory changes and trends in compliance issues is vital for successful implementation of an ESOP in companies to achieve the objectives. ESOP has to be a structured as part of the total compensation strategy. Retention and attraction of key talents can be achieved through ESOP.

While ESOP is extremely useful best practice, failure
to communicate, educate and make people understand the intricacies can leave the employees highly disappointed.

7. Leadership Influence on Employee Motivation and Retention.

In this chapter, we understand about the impact of leadership on the morale of followers and the effect on the teamwork. There are always instances of exemplary leadership which had raised the bar very high to enlist, encourage from the heart and enable their subordinates to excel and succeeded. How the leaders are able to use the reward and recognition to inspire excellence is worth emulating. There are numerous examples of leadership failures and unethical and unprincipled behaviour for personal gains as well. One case example is detailed here for the purpose of driving home the point of leadership connection to employee morale. Some of the unique endowments of such leaders who plan and drive recognition are also outlined.

In any sphere of activity, be it business, politics or nation building, an effective leadership can galvanize the efforts of people, unify and motivate towards the goal.

Leadership is the ability to enable people to do what one wants them to do willingly to realise any super ordinary goal.
Leadership which is an action, can be defined as
$L=f(l, f, s)$.
Leadership is dependent on three variables.

Leader's Personality.

The personality type of two leaders is never the same. Every leader is unique in the thinking, feeling and behaving especially in a given situation. In the workplaces, leader's style has telling and lasting influence on people.

The issue that arises often while talking about leadership is the degree of influence of the personality of the leader and the leadership effectiveness?"

Is there one personality type that can be effective in most situations? Leadership effectiveness is not totally independent of personality. The role of personality in leadership cannot be brushed aside as personality impacts leader's performance.

Personality drives the natural tendency to act in a situation.

It is imperative for leaders understand their own personality in order to be effective, as there is a close relationship between followers' perception of personality of their leader and the leaders overall performance effectiveness depends on that perception.

Whenever the followers accepted and believed a person to be great leader, the person did have few key personality traits. The personality factors which closely affected the performance are the dependability, agreeableness, emotional stability, intellectual ability and urgency. (Big five factors) * Several studies have found that leadership effectiveness and the big five personality traits are closely correlated.

A specific study found that executives who assumed leadership role at Sears had all these five personality factors. This study also revealed that the perception of the leader by the team members played a significant role in leader's performance and the entire team's performance. In another study involving the airline cabin crew found that an aggressive, emotionally unstable captain could not ensure efficient crew performance and many errors were committed by the crew.

Persuading the team members to keep aside their personal preferences and work towards a common goal is natural the leaders were emotionally stable knows about two great leaders and both were successful even though they had totally different personalities. The personality of Steve jobs of Apple is something that many would like to copy He was known to be an ENTJ but unlike many of this type. He was dominating, highly passionate, loved challenges and always insisted on perfection in execution from his team and followers at times, making it impossible for many to work with him. His personality was very unpredictable and many hated him for his total disrespect for disagreement from anyone.

Tim Cook on the contrary was calm and cool personality. He had complete faith in the capability of others. Always respected the feelings of people around. Unlike Steve, who fanned passion for new products, Tim maintained his focus on higher order values. The personality of these two and their leadership styles, though different had the greatest influence in creating world's richest business empire.

The followers Maturity:

When operating with teams the members may be at various levels of maturity in their ability to execute –skill- and their willingness to voluntarily execute the task-attitude. This dimension of the followers has telling effect on the effectiveness. If the leader's style is inflexible and one dimensional the effectiveness is bound to be lost.

The situation and the task.

The leadership cannot be effective if the approach is one of a total delegation when there is a crisis. Unique style for all levels and situations unmindful of the urgency of the task on hand cannot deliver.

When the profits are dropping quarter after quarter, and there is cash crunch either a pay cut or lay off along with a suspension of all rewards is required to be done.

An analysis of the organization and the top management style will enable the understanding of leaders' role in dealing with the situations.

As the saying goes, it is the people who fail the system and the system never fails. If it is not the ineffectiveness of leadership what else, then causes the untimely death of successful business organizations?

Bear Stearns and Barings bank despite a glorious history were destroyed by the employees who exploited the system that provided for huge rewards.

Is it excessive greed and hunger for windfall reward money, poor risk management systems, inadequate or lack of governance, a weak Board with low conviction and the lack of diversity in business mix, or combination of all of the above?

The Classic case of leadership failure:

Bear Stearns does not fall among the Wall Street elite financial giants. It was the fifth-biggest investment bank and was perceived as outlier. The leadership legacy includes people who had a passion for sports and games. One need not be a Harvard or Yale graduate to be the CEO.

Nero was supposed to have been fiddling when Rome was burning, but a modern-day Wall Street investment bank's CEO actually went one step further. When Bear Stearns was burning the CEO Jimmy Cayne, who had led the bank for nearly two decades successfully was playing bridge which he always enjoyed doing than the CEO Job.

He had worked his way up from a travelling salesman. He had sold scrap iron and municipal bonds besides few other jobs.

He was hired as a stockbroker at Bear Stearns because of his expertise in the game of bridge by the new friend, he acquired. Later on, Cayne earned his position in 1985 as the CEO.

He became the CEO and remained until January 2008 to become the longest-serving CEO. He built his wealth and the company's wealth of billions. Being in the leadership role, his easy going life and leadership style did have a high influence on the followers but when the situation demanded the leadership style did not effectively work as he did not take charge to stop or control the unbridled enthusiasm of his executives who were driven by greed to earn huge rewards.

In the past Bear Stearns had survived threats like the Great Depression, Black Monday and the Eleven Nine crises, but could not shake away and survive the bad and high-risk bets by its leaders.

In March 2008, Bear Stearns had piled up huge commitments on toxic mortgages.

In a very short span of just weeks, Bear Stearns ran out of cash and two days later was forced to agree to a government backed sale, to JP Morgan Chase. Bear Stearns shares had tumbled from $ 173 $ to $ 1 and its past glory of growth history of 85 years did not help.

The Culture shock:

At Bear Stearns the tone for aggressiveness, to be more tactical than strategic and profit only motive was set by Alan Greenburg the earliest chairman.

The culture rewarded the risk takers amply and their crazy risk-taking behaviour without having adequate accountability whatsoever.

Bear Stearns rose to be the country's fifth biggest investment bank and was the recipient of Wall Street's most-admired financial firms. It always hired smart people and operated in cutting-edge and complex financial instrument market. The tempo was always ultra-competitive culture at Bear Stearns. It was a place with a lot of "sharp elbows" with people competing to get ahead and to make lots of money.

It did not matter for Bear Stearns even if someone had failed miserably in previous job, they would hire people who had failed elsewhere.

Their preference was not for MBA or Ivy League school students, but for poor, smart and a deep desire to become rich candidates. Bear Stearns built up a very aggressive culture by hiring people who were hungry for getting rich quickly.

The weak leadership isn't the only reason for Bear Stearns to be sold for a paltry sum to avoid being bankrupt. The conflict and differing opinions among other senior executives contributed to the calamity.

Alan Schwartz, who took over as CEO from Cayne in early 2008 always wrong picture that Bear Stearns did not have any cash problem causing damage to the company.

There were intense conflicts with Cayne causing more damage to the operations and control.

Initially, Cayne was successful to get the stock price to surge from about $16 to $173 through his leadership when he took over as CEO in 1993. When the fire sale agreement came the deal was initially at $1.

Rewarding Corporate Murder:

When Bear Stearns was in death bed every finance company in the Wall Street from small to big land at Bear Stearns doors to scavenge on people. Bear Stearns executives are now occupying high paying jobs in every company in Wall Street.

Five years after the collapse of Bear Stearns executives who were in the middle of that calamity ended up holding more lucrative jobs with better pay and benefits and more power.

Wall-Street giants like JP Morgan, Goldman Sachs, Bank of America, and Deutsche Bank ironically had poached many of the senior executives.

Through the leadership these men had destroyed $19.1 trillion wealth of common people and cost as many as 8.8 million jobs, 10000 of the 14000 employees ended up with the pink slip while their bosses landed big jobs.

There were arguments in their favour that they got rewarded for the high-risk they took. They got the best pay and did not pay for the consequences for their decisions.

Thomas Marano was given a pay more than $29 million, as head of Residential Capital, LLC.GMAC ended up facing bail out by the government during the crisis.

Marano's house is spread over 4,700 square feet in New Jersey and he also occupies a vacation home in Park City, Utah. Later Old Pike Associates II, LLC, which was formed in March 2012, had Morano as the head the company bought for him a $4.1 million dollar home Marano's pay was at 8 million, including liberal stock options. Marano's direct report Jeffrey Verschleiser ended up having a senior job at Goldman Sache. A house ten million dollar million is abode of Jeffrey Verschleiser home at The Fifth Avenue apartment in New York City.

Michael Nierenberg has an upscale place to live in the New York City suburb of Port Washington and work at Bank of America Nierenberg headed function of adjustable rate mortgage and collateralized debt obligation desks at Bear Stearns, and heads the mortgages and securitized products at Bank of America after the collapse

His acquisitions include over six million worth house with every amenity one can think of and boat dock.

Silverstein was joint head of mortgage finance and later continued at JPMorgan for a short time after the acquisition.

Later on, moving to Bank of America as managing director. Silverstein has a lavish style of living in $3.7 million waterfront home swimming pool and tennis court.

Mary Haggerty was heading mortgage finance portfolio at Bear. Her major initiative was a cut back on the due diligence processes its mortgage-backed securities to induce a competitive edge on bids from larger sub-prime sellers. She became the managing director in the securitized products group after the acquisition by JP Morgan. Mary Haggerty too possessed million-dollar apartment in New York City. Mayer took up the job at Swiss banking giant UBS in 2008. After Two years he joined The Deutsche Bank and headed corporate banking and securities in North America.

The people who were supposed to lead and setting an example and be the most responsible have never paid a penny for their leadership failure but gained personally substantial wealth.

The American management gurus continue to preach principle-cantered leadership, but the Wall Street executives seem to be proving that nothing but money and greed matters.

As in the previous occasions, the regulatory actions against an even handful of those individuals who were in positions of power during the financial crisis do not seem to have deterred anyone.

Twenty-two years and five financial crises later, the men in Wall Street are right back at high-risk games for reward of huge monetary gains and lavish life. Having said that, the leadership effectiveness definitely depends on the spontaneity and having a heart to give credit to the followers. Spontaneity and creativity besides simplicity is the characteristics of exemplary leaders. Here are instances of the leader's spontaneity.

Hewlett-Packard has been encouraging Inventive spirit and they have institutionalized the very prestigious honours, for employees. Reportedly, it all started with an indent when an employee working on a difficult problem found a creative solution and could not hide the happiness.

He then rushed into his boss's cabin to announce the solution he found for that long-standing problem.

The manager was obviously thrilled, but spontaneously wanted to acknowledge the effort. He could find only a banana that was left over to give his subordinate as an instant appreciation. This got institutionalized and till today, the employees cherish this award as the greatest accomplishment.

AT&T and Employee Recognition: The African philosophy of Ubuntu (driving mutual respect and tolerance) perhaps been institutionalized AT AT&T.

The leadership encourages the employees always to express the gratitude by saying "Thank You" to everyone who was helpful.

Thanking is simple yet very powerful way to create a culture of respect for each other. It ensures better performance through collaboration in unexpected ways.

People are encouraged to develop the habit of acknowledging someone who helps in the work. A message of thanks to someone can be written by using a special sheet of coloured paper officially provided.

Employees had written over 130,000 thank you notes in four-year span. The culture had set in and got transformed when the management intervened to spur that hidden need through the recognition program.

Walt Disney World: When it comes to finding ways to recognize employees no one can beat Walt Disney.

Their Employee recognition portfolio has over 180 different recognition programs. "The award was named after Fred, reflecting the true spirit of someone who had risen from the lowest rank by living and espousing company values.

The highlight of the award is the certificate mounted on a plaque and the bronze statuette of Mickey Mouse. They were awarded to any employee to reflect and cherish the values.

Walt Disney runs the world's busiest and successful theme parks. Disney theme park generated more than $700 million in profits since opening in 1992 and made $85.7 million in 2015.

Totally they attracted 132.5 million guests and every day when the gates open, adults and children alike are eagerly waiting to seek the happiness and it is the employees behind the costumes who spread happiness without disappointment.

Disney had immense love for drawing and he loved animals which he later on turned into the successful business vision and philosophy of spreading entertainment and happiness.

He was obsessed with creating the happiest Place on earth, though he had an unhappy childhood as his father had a violent temper and beat his children regularly. Disney found happiness by immersing himself in drawings and found his own dream world to escape. The secrets to this success lie in the way Disney's value of happiness generation. This is institutionalized into unique culture through its employee recognition programs.

The secret behind Disney's theme park's profit is its obsessive culture of happiness that is contagious. While every other business goes after profit, Disney believes in promoting intangibles and they firmly believe that profit flows from that.

That huge success of the Walt Disney Empire is purely by living the values of being friendly, resourceful, enthusiastic and dependable. Disney's mission of creating happiness is very simple but powerful.

Initiating new habits:

There are numerous companies in the world that are classified as most hazardous workplaces. When following safety instructions became the issue, the leadership had to find ways to constantly remind and encourage behaviour of safe working.

To recharge and energize their safety program, they instituted an award which consisted of a recharged gift-card. If the employees are to be motivated to take a simple step towards safety improvement, like attending a safety meeting, fire drill or first aid one needs to be creative in changing habits of people. To improve safety habits the leaders found a way to do this by letting people earn points for every step towards positive safety related contribution. Those points could later be redeemed for choice gifts.

The simple idea to accumulate the points has motivated many employees to do the right thing towards safe operations. The accident rate after they initiated this reward declined significantly. Handling a merger creative way to Reward: When any company is seeking accelerated growth, merger and acquisition becomes the best option.

The merger can be the most difficult and daunting task, especially for HR, as bringing the integration of two different cultures quickly is always tough and the skills to lead the integration are tested to the hilt. When two giant pharmaceutical companies were merging the whole job, challenge was assigned to a task force for making the transition a smooth affair. Their goal was to complete the project in six months.

Their creative approach helped the team members achieved the goal and were rewarded in a way for working late hours, and going beyond the call duty with unique gifts which were one of a lifetime.

The recipient got a personalized card with a letter from the supervisor, and the reward money could be used to buy a variety of services like house cleaning, lawn care, carpet cleaning, and even pest control.

The impact is felt by the family as well.

People are respected, and performance is nurtured in RMSI, a company which provides IT services with thousand employees. This small company dislodged Google, which always topped as the best employer in India.

They place a premium on high level of empowerment, mentoring and coaching. The program of corporate social responsibility is the biggest USP of RMSI. Apart from rewarding individual efforts, the reward and recognition programs ensure that team efforts are also rewarded. Innovation, creativity, leadership skills are also rewarded.

8. The Most Preferred Employers.

Inthis chapter, we dive deeper into what the top ten and the next twenty of the globally most preferred employers do, to remain at the top of the chart. Many of the best HR practices are also detailed.

When it comes to making the most likable places to work, it is the leadership and company values espoused that matters to the highest degree. The power of the vision does matter as it happened with Steve job's vision for Apple. By being a visionary leader, one can earn enormous respect from employees and make them love the organization.

The technology companies appear to practice these things very easily accompanied by consumer product and retail companies. One leader with a vision made all the difference in companies like Amazon, Apple, and Google. By being closer to customers, these companies have always created the "moments of truth" for employees.

The parent company's core values which drive the policies, systems, and processes have effectively influenced the culture globally in companies like Microsoft,

Google and Intuit are the Indian companies similar to Godrej, Mahindra, and the Oberoi Hotels who have succeeded in creating their own version of great places to work. If one looks at the list of top ten and next twenty companies in India, it can be seen that they do a few things very well to make the workplace the most admired one.

About fifty per cent of the most liked companies in India are known to have an ESOP plan in place; forty per cent provides housing benefits; fifty per cent or more provide credit card, mobile phones as perks. There is a reported case of a privately owned company which buys.

Most admired Indian companies and how their core values drive and motivate people.

Name of the company-- Employee Strength --The best practices

Google India-1, 700--Does not hire stereotypes--abundant communication--fun at work.

American Express India--10,400--Flexibility at work--cross-functional opportunities.

Ujjain Financial Services--7,800--No designations-ESOP.

Teleperformance India--4,600--Values-get inspired and be proud.

Godrej Consumer Products--1,200-- Empowerment, recognition, happy work environment.

Marriott Hotels India--8200--Global growth opportunities-- no hierarchy

SAP Labs India-5, 339-challenging work--top pay benefits.

The Oberoi Group Hotel/Resort--4,000--customer delights as value--employee empowerment.

Lemon Tree Hotels--1,768--culture of fulfilling aspirations.

Intuit India--6,700--fostering a collaborative culture.

Hyatt Hotels & Resorts--Value driven--Listen and learn.

Cadence Design Systems--1,500—drive, passion for work.

PayPal India Pvt Ltd--1,000-- collaboration-innovation-wellness-inclusion.

Federal Express Corporation--5,800-People-Service-Profit-Philosophy.

Intercontinental Hotels Group--5, 200--do right--care for guest—celebrations--make a difference--Work well together.

Blue Dart Express-- 9,900-- Customer Excellence.

DHL Express (India) -- 1,400--customer centric –delivery excellences.

Mahindra & Mahindra Automotive & Farm Equipment--9200- growth and development

Cisco Systems (India) –-- 9,300--win together- care for each other.

Adobe Systems India--3,800--Be genuine-exceptional-innovative-involved.

Standard Chartered-- Scope International--12,000--Employee welfare.

Microsoft India-- 7, 000--Growth mind-set-customer obsession.

Hilton Worldwide--1,000--innovation-quality-success

Shriram Value Services--1,800--client satisfaction-professionalism-technical competence.

Mahindra Intertrade--150--development- collaborative works

Classic Stripes--500--customer focus-- seeking feedback-empowerment.

Pitney Bowes Software India--500--Innovation

NTPC Ltd --22,000--Customer focus- organizational pride- innovation and learning- total quality-safety.

In India the best places to work are dominated by the technology sector and lead the way, followed by consumer product sector and then the retail sector. Hospitality industry also had a sizable number of the best place to work.

Dream companies to work in the USA -2015.

It is the technology sector that leads in the number of most preferred employers in the USA also.

An exterior home renovation company, Power Home Remodelling of Pennsylvania took the No. 1 spot and what they offered was career opportunities for the employees.

The best-known IT companies in the USA were Google, Apple, Allied wallet, Twitter. Next best sector was financial services. Retail and real estate also had a fair share of ideal organizations to work.

As per survey conducted in 2016 by LinkedIn Alphabet, Google's found the top place. In second place was Amazon, the Seattle, Washington-based internet company whose online shopping platform, media and cloud business.

Worldwide, the company employs about 341,400 people. Third place was occupied by Facebook, another highly largest networking company in the world, with 1.9 billion monthly users. The firm also owns WhatsApp and Instagram.

More than 168,000 undergraduate students responded to the survey in 2015 choosing Europe's most preferred employers. The top five ideal employers seem to be IBM, BMW, Siemens, Google, and Microsoft. "Companies ranked higher in the European survey continue to deliver strong and attractive communication to prospects across all markets. "This is not easy as the European market consists of a complex group of cultures with varying expectations," observed Claudia Tattanelli, Chairman Strategic Board at Universum Global.

Top consulting services companies like KPMG, PWC and CBA, focused on offering flexible working schedules and few unique perks to reach top rank as the most preferred employers. Flexibility seems to be the most popular approach across the Australia.

The companies compete with each other to offer the best flexibility," By default they offer opportunities for remote working or non-standard hours of work

Australian employees are offered the flexibility of scheduling four long days instead of five regular working days or working for three days in the office and two from home. Another innovative idea of making employees to choose work-place was experimented by Westpac that resulted in valuable savings.

Australian employers offered the most competitive perks of all employers globally. After having a baby, the new parent could avail of 4-day work week in Vodafone.

This was a very liberal parental benefit Qantas and Virgin Australia rewarded employees heavily discounted flights. Companies offering domestic violence support are uniquely common to Australia.

KPMG, PwC, Deloitte, Commonwealth Bank of Australia, Bank of Queensland, Medibank, Vodafone, Australia, Quantas, and Virgin Australia are among the best employers.

Few specific Examples of unique rewards:

These are mere suggestive ideas. Many of them were successfully implemented with one hundred per cent achievement of the end results. These parameters need to be customized to suit the organization culture, the size and budget.

Vital points to make implementation successful:

There will always be criticism of lack of objectivity. To overcome it is suggested to have a committee to decide on the awards. While constituting the committee, have one representative of employees besides representation from other levels to increase transparency and reduce accusations of bias.

All the eligible and recommended names must be placed before the Committee, which should discuss all nominations for every award. Every member should cast their vote for selection.

Award Name: Pat on the back.

Frequency: whenever an event happens-the number of awards restricted at 10% of the total population.

Type: Spot Award.

Criteria: Any team supportive actions by team member identified through peer nominations or manager's nomination

Value: $5 or IRs.100 a gourmet coffee shop gift card.

Process owner-Manager/ HR.

Award Name: Most cooperative Team.

Frequency-- Monthly.

The Supervisor is empowered to give spot awards; the number is limited and reward for own team members. Variation is to allow managers without team/direct report to nominate members of another team.

Who is eligible? --All employees.

Criteria: Going beyond assigned job responsibility – Enhancing Company image and brand-- customer delight – Helping team member to solve any issues.

Type of Reward-- $ 20 /Rs.100 gift card and letter of appreciation l-- manager personally hands over the award to the team member.

Process Owner-- HR-- maintains Record.

Frequency: Semi--Annual.

Total awards- limited to 4 awards in one year.

Eligibility--All employees.

Criteria: An exhibition of extraordinary technical skills; taking initiative to solve difficult technical problem.

Supervisor Nominates and Reward Committee will decide.

Type: Long innings /Service oriented.

Eligibility-- Full-time employees who complete landmark years like five, ten or even fifteen years of continuous service.

Type and Value--$500 IRS 5000/10000/25000- for family outing within the country for 10 years and above outside the country

Additional paid vacation-- to be used within one year of completion date

Process Owner-- HR.

Award Type--: Event milestone in Employee's Personal life.

Criteria: employee's Marriage/Childbirth.

Eligibility-- All Employees.

A Gift of flowers or Gift card – value $50 to 100 /IRS.1500.00 to IRS.2000/-

An employee informs HR who administers Budget-

Frequency – As and when an event occurs.

Eligibility-- Only to employees and not managers.

Criteria--Iconic award given to one or two employees in the whole company, who exhibit all around loyalty, radiate and propagate values, promote the company image and do extraordinary things to help others. Win peer admiration and exhibit exemplary leadership qualities

Selection Process: A manager nominates one subordinate and final recipient is decided by a committee through open voting. The manager who nominates has to justify his nomination in the meeting.

Type and Value: Cash award $500/Rs.5000/-to be spent for any external training nomination approved by the HR manager

Process owner: HR

Frequency: Annual

Criteria: Emerging leaders displaying visible leadership qualities,

Pro-activeness, company value alignment, leading business initiatives, cohesive teamwork, etc.

Eligibility--All employees

Nomination by reporting manager:

Process owner: HR.

Type: Annual-cash-not exceeding $100 or IRS 5000.00

Category-- Individual.

Criteria – Exhibition of leadership qualities

Increased paid time off: Unlike fixed paid time-off policies that prevailed the trend is to reward exceptionally good performers with additional PTO. These days finding personal time has become more valuable.

Flexible hours: Typical eight hours of working at stretch have given way to flexible working hours. Management, especially in IT industry, is more flexible with flexible hours.

Telecommuting/Remote working: With the advent of high-speed internet technology, one does not need to be physically being in office.

Oracle and similar companies have been encouraging telecommuting. This is a very valuable benefit for many working couples.

Employee Health and Wellness: Reward programs now aim at maintaining health of employees by paying for fitness club membership and even extended break hours or Gymnasium in the office.

Social networking butterfly: Company sponsored learning events in social networks have become powerful types of rewards.

Praising in Facebook, LinkedIn I also another form called social butterfly.

Bonus points plan: Similar to credit card usage points, employees are encouraged to accumulate bonus points for expected behaviour and redeem it for certain wellness benefits or a learning opportunity.

Wall of Fame:

Each group creates a wall of fame and posts picture of the employee for extraordinary contribution as determined by the team and posts in their workplace or even at the head office where everyone can see. In the glass factory experiment cited above, we had tried having at the work station a placard with the employee's picture and the data about the highest production he achieved. This really worked wonders on the person.

Family welfare:

Google did have a reward that should be emulated by other companies. In case of death of an employee, the spouse or domestic partner receives fifty per cent of the salary, irrespective of the length of service. Payment is made every year for the next decade.

Free mentoring for fast track: Everyone wants to enhance the promotion chance, but do not know what to improve. HR can offer free mentoring for a specific period from a senior executive to those identified for recognition.

Free tuition /sabbatical leave:

Companies that encourage knowledge update either sponsor for a course. Or allow employees to take unpaid leave with guarantee for employment

Best Team Effort.

The criteria- Team should have been on one project

Team size limited to a minimum of three and maximum of twenty the team should have exhibited team cohesion; support for team members is evident in day to day task, Project delivery on time.

Selection process: The entire team makes a presentation to the selection panel for 15 minutes highlighting why they should be given the award and every member must speak in well-coordinated manner.

The award: The winning team gets IRS.2000 per member. The maximum award amount limited to IRS.25000. The team must collectively decide the mode of spending and no cash draws were allowed.

Appendix 1

Key Concepts

Asclepiades

Asclepiades also referred to as Asclepiades of Bithynia or Asclepiades of Prusa was a physician and native of Prusias-on-Sea in Bithynia in Asia Minor and had practice at Rome. Near the end of the 2nd century BC, the Greek system of medicine was established by him.

Like modern day revolutionary thinkers, this ancient doctor who preached the therapeutic benefits of wine and passive exercise was widely admired and followed by many.

However, Asclepiades of Bithynia was ahead of his time and went beyond traditional ways. He developed an extraordinary theory which was the foundation for new normal and was called Methodism. He was ridiculed and condemned by his community and friends.

Most of his work got destroyed, but few reconstructed facts offer glimpse of how Hellenistic philosophy and medicine interacted.

Appendix 2

Key Jargons

Abenomics expansion:

The term refers to the economic revival strategy of the Japanese Prime Minister Shinzō Abe.

Appraisal:

Normally used as a tool for assessment of an employee's performance on the job and for providing feedback. This process is conducted by the immediate supervisor, once a year. Variations include more frequent and shorter versions as HR best practice. There are multiple methods like the confidential and close-ended reporting to the open ended 180 degree and 360-degree processes.

Apprentice:

This refers to the people who are hired to receive on the job training while they are doing their technical courses either a diploma or undergraduate study. Government and Many private technical institutes provide the skill-based education and these candidates are selected normally as apprentice.

Bonus:

The bonus is over and above the normal annual pay for better performance. The amount is based on the individual's performance and the company's profit. There is a legal obligation for compulsory distribution of profits in India.

Culture:

The ideas, norms and patterns of social behaviour in any society. In the organizational context culture refers to the unique common behaviour patterns of employees. The top leadership 's behaviour sets the tone, especially of the founders and the principles in their everyday walk of the talk creates the culture.

Employee Engagement:

This refers to the commitment level of employees to the organization, its philosophy, vision and values. The engagement level and the number of people who are engaged determines the organizational effectiveness and high retention

Incentive:

Incentives are motivational tools used to encourage higher performance Not long ago the Indian cricket players could aspire to play in local Ranji Trophy cricket matches and very few made to national as the players got paid paltry sums. These days with introduction of Indian Premier League the players are paid few million and the result is flood of high calibre players. Definitely the incentive paid huge role in motivating young talents to choose cricket as a career in a society where this was a taboo. Incentives are given in the form of commission, stock options or pay hike. The incentive plans are created for a one-year period, tied up with annual targets while rewards are of shorter time frame. Incentives rules are made up front for a year and communicated to target group of employees. The incentive is what causes the effect of reward.

Layoff:
Companies in India rarely resort to this form of temporary termination of labour for reasons of lack of work, severe cash or material shortages

Misconduct: Misconduct in employment is deliberate violation of rules and regulations. Depending on the type of misconduct and the severity of the act, the punishments are determined. Typically for all major misconducts a departmental enquiry is must.

Reward:

The Reward is the monetary or non-monetary return for giving outstanding performance. For many years when any Indian athlete did remarkably well, the reward was only few thousand rupees. Off late when the reward money is raised to a few millions, suddenly there are many medal winners in the Olympics and other world cup sports events. Women have entered in large numbers to win and this can be attributed to the cash rewards.

Recognition:

It is similar to Ubuntu - the positive acknowledgment- of good contribution. Recognition is primarily used to give that psychological stroke which gives emotional satisfaction.
It is not uncommon to set up specified standards of attainment. Recognition must be given even for the smallest achievements even if it is in the personal context.
When you recognize someone, it is like breathing life and proving the very existence. Just as breathing, recognition has been life supporting.

Stock:

A company, whether privately owned or publicly owned, raises money through subscription to various types of shares which is also called stock. Shares can be held by owner or promoters or even public. Companies whose shares are listed on the stock exchange are public companies. Employees are also given Stocks in appreciation of their loyalty or contribution /risk

Termination

This is when a job contract ends. This can be voluntary or involuntary. Employment termination can be for a cause

Appendix 3

Important Labour laws in India

This section is created especially for HR professionals in multinational companies having Indian operations or start-ups planning to set- up offshore base in India. One can get a comprehensive view of the labour laws is presented here along with

Brief history and genesis of the Indian Labour laws.

The British influence can be seen on The Indian labour laws which were mainly established and fine-tuned to suit British political and economic conditions and to protect the commercial interests of British employers.

The Factories Act was introduced first, as a result of pressure brought by British textile magnates for their selfish interest to prevent the competition from India that had plenty of intelligent and hardworking cheap labour force.

It was common practice for British colonial owners of textile mills to exploit workers by making male and female workers to work for extended hours without overtime and deploy even minors.

The Factories Act started to restore some order amidst chaos by prescribing limits on working hours, employment of children and tried to curb work timings for women especially in night shifts.

The overtime wage payments for working beyond eight hours were brought in. These were significant steps even though it benefitted British business interests.

This was followed by more laws on Forced Labour in the year 1930. Abolition of Forced Labour in 1957, Equal Remuneration in 1951 and Discrimination (employment and occupation) in 1958 were the legal measures taken subsequently. These were laws that addressed welfare of workers and prevention of unfair labour practices.

Trade unionism and the Trade Union Act 1926 came in to empower workers for collective bargaining mechanism. Even today there are ten major central union organizations of workers based on different political ideologies and every state or local union is affiliated to one of these.

The All India Trade Union Congress (AITUC) was the pioneering setup created in 1920, almost three decades before India became independent.

The working class all over the world has fought for the freedom of association as the fundamental right. Many laws have guaranteed this right under the Constitution of that country. The Trade Union Act was enacted to ensure that right. However, the irony is that even if a union manages to get registered, it does not guarantee that the employer will recognize the union as a sole bargaining agent. There is in fact no law which compels a management to recognize a trade union and consequently there is no legal compulsion for employers, even in the organized sector, to enter into collective bargaining. The advocates of best business practices however resort to a negotiated settlement. It is not uncommon to see managements resorting to encouraging inter union or multiple union rivalries to keep them at bay. Therefore, any union even with a handful of members tries to flex the muscle and show off the strength.

For example, the history of Union militancy was at its peak during the mammoth textile strike of Bombay. In late 1981, Bombay's Textile workers who had been with Indian Trade Union Congress decided to choose Dutta Samant, another militant trade union leader, which led to the head on collision with the Bombay Mill Owners Association.

The textile industry of the city was up in arms and eventually the mill owners decided to shut down leaving 250,000 workers jobless. All because of one man's power hunger. The demand was wage hikes, besides demand for scrapping of the Bombay Industrial Act of 1947. Fighting for greater pay and better conditions for the workers, Samant and his allies also were at the power control game. Backed by the Political bigwig the strike had telling effect on every walk of life of Bombay.

Sensing the political ambitions of the Union leader the then prime minister Indira Gandhi decided to reject all the demands and this resulted in many people committing suicide, besides loss of job for thousands. There is no better example of the misuse of freedom by union leaders for their own political ambitions.

How wages are controlled to ensure fair treatment.

Wage determination for workers in India has been driven mainly through the Employee's compensation act 1923 (workmen's compensation Act) and The Minimum Wages Act 1948.
The Payment of wages Act, Equal remuneration act, and other laws which regulate the payment of compensation.

Handling the strikes and lockouts in India.

The tendency of Labour Unions and the Workers is to resort to stoppage of work very often though the law requires a formal notice to the management.
Disrupting the daily life and creating huge economic losses has been the main weapon for forcing managements to increase wages.
As India is trying to liberalize and privatize to build a strong economy by injecting private participation, there are multiple political forces who work against the initiative of the government. Especially in a multi-party democratic system the political will over shadows economic considerations while creating the welfare state. The willingness or conviction of political leaders to see their party's ideologies and principles which they publicly advocated and promised to gain votes, and how they actually get implemented, and achieves the results in the way promised, is a test of the strength of the political will.
Be it Donald Trump or Narendra Modi, who parted from the tradition to push their ideas, could achieve their objectives only due

to sheer dogmatism. The leftist Trade unions in India have the tendency to oppose anything and everything that ruling party attempts.

The number of irrelevant issues brought in the Indian parliament to disrupt the proceedings is an indication of the political chaos that can be created in a parliamentary democracy.

In 2012 and in September 2016, millions of employees of government -run banks, government offices and factories were closed as people protested against price rise, government's economic policies and plans to privatize. Bank employees, school teachers, postal workers, miners and construction workers, were among the crowd demanding the dropping of privatization initiative.

It is not uncommon for employers resort to the extreme measure of a lockout as final step whenever there is prolonged strike or violence the government appointed conciliation officers facilitate the negotiated settlement. The irony is that conciliation efforts are not legally binding on the parties.

If the dispute still remains unresolved, the federal government may intervene and refer the dispute adjudication process and may even ban the strike or lockout.

The Industrial Disputes Act 1947 is the law that addresses legally, any dispute between management and workers or unions. Any modification to the existing service conditions cannot be done unilaterally and notice of 21 days to the workers and the union is required to be given.

Similarly, during the pendency of dispute before an authority under the IDA, the previous service conditions in respect of that dispute cannot be altered without prior permission of the government authority concerned if this involves any disadvantage to the workers. This extent of rigidity in labour laws has had limiting influence on foreign direct investment till recently. The changes in some of those laws have however been attracting big global companies.

Handling the termination or removal of employee from the service.

In the existing constitutional framework, the right to earn livelihood is paramount. Therefore, involuntary termination of employment is next to impossible unless someone commits serious misconduct like fraud, misappropriation. Even assault can escape termination. Reasons of chronic and prolonged absenteeism, drug and alcoholism, severe health conditions resulting in disability, old age are not even sufficient grounds to terminate the services of an employee.

Any discipline related issues must follow the set procedure of issuing show cause notice, charge sheet, domestic enquiry and the award of a punishment. If an employee is proved to have engaged in any form of misconduct, there are various levels of punishment for different types of misconducts and the departmental inquiry is mandatory for establishing major misconducts and the process must follow the principles of 'natural justice'. Even the verdict after the enquiry can be challenged in court of law.

If the punitive verdict by the inquiry officer is dismissal, based on the inquiry findings, the verdict can be challenged in the courts. The court verdict goes generally in favour of the employees with reinstatement and continuity of service, back wages and consequential benefits in almost every case; it takes twenty to twenty-five years of legal process for the final verdict in Supreme Court which is the final appellate court.

Hiring temporary workers can be done through registered contractors under The Contract Labour (Prohibition and Regulation) Act 1970. There are many court rulings in favour of absorption of contract labour if management employs the same person for extended periods, and this has created a huge anomaly about hiring people on contract.

The workplace accidents and the compensation to be paid are covered under Workman's compensation Act, one of the main legislations which cover all cases of workplace accidents.

Employees State Insurance Scheme provides for loss of compensation, medical treatment at low rates.

The act provides for an insurance cover where the employer and the employee contribute a percentage of the monthly wage.

The Corporation runs dispensaries and hospitals in working class localities providing for outpatient and in-patient care and freely dispenses medicines and covers hospitalization needs and costs. This is very unique and very important welfare benefit.

Employment injury, including occupational disease is compensated according to a schedule of rates proportionate to the extent of injury and loss of earning capacity.

Payment, unlike in the Workmen's Compensation Act. Despite the laudable objective and tight supervision of the running of the scheme, the entire scheme has degenerated due to corruption and inefficiency. Workers in need of genuine medical attention are reluctant to use it. Progressive managements have gone for private group medical insurances to give better deals.

Two types of retirement benefit, generally is available. The Payment of Gratuity Act and the Provident Fund Act. These two laws ensure substantial retirement pay-out.

The law and Employed Women.

Though India has a large illiterate Women population, they constitute a significant part of the workforce in the organized and unorganized sector.

They are treated differently in most workplaces in employment terms. According to Government sources out of the ninety million are women workers, a large percentage of about eighty-seven percentage is in the agricultural sector. Construction sector as daily wage labourers. In urban areas, the employment of women in the organized sector is better off in terms of gender discrimination Apart from the Maternity Benefit Act, almost all the major central labour laws are applicable to women workers. The Equal Remuneration Act passed in 1976 ensures non-discrimination of women in the payment of wages. The Factories act prohibits woman from working from seven p. m till 6 am. However few states amended the rules to permit woman to work till 10 p. m though few court rulings have created conflicting judgments.

The Ministry of Labour of the central government assumed the responsibility to protect and safeguard the interests of workers. The Ministry constantly is in consultation with chambers of commerce, trade unions, and business heads to achieve the objective by enacting

employment of workers. Various labour laws in the areas of wage policies, minimum wages, employment service, vocational training, and workers' education, have been either replaced or modified recently thereby removing the old legacy of British rulers.

Major Amendments in labour laws.

Maternity Benefit Act.

The paid maternity leave was raised to twenty-six weeks placing India among the top three countries in generosity of maternity benefits.

The Indian government legislated with Persons with Disabilities Act. The persons with disabilities are given adequate protection by this law and the act aligns with the principles of the United Nations Convention on the Rights of Persons with Disabilities.

Health benefit to workers

Indian government ensures the benefit of health care through a social insurance scheme. Through this participatory scheme hospital benefits are also made available to the workers.

The threshold salary for eligible employees under the Employees' State Insurance Act, 1948 was raised by 60% to provide medical coverage to a wider section of factories and other establishment employees.

In a move to simplify certain labour law compliance, paperwork was considerably reduced from fifty-six to five and also the number of records employers had to maintain fewer than nine. The ease of doing business with government departments was not at all easy and that has been considerably improved with the

e governance initiatives by the government agencies.

The Factories Act:

This act regulates normal working hours for adult workers in factories to nine hours per day and forty-eight hours per week. Any worker who has worked for two hundred and forty days can get paid time off of twelve working days. Workers are entitled to pay days-off during public and religious festivals, including memorial and religious holidays.

As per the Indian constitution, there are only three mandatory holidays which are Republic Day (January 26), Independence Day (August 15) and Gandhi Jayanti (October 2).

The Trade Unions Act.

The procedure for registration of a Trade Union and its conduct is prescribed in the Indian Trade Unions Act and in The Industrial disputes Act and also for raising disputes for any wage related issues or unfair labour practices.

The right to strike and collective bargaining is protected under ID Act and Trade unions act. Though the unions cannot resort to sudden strike action and are required to give six weeks' notice, it is not uncommon to see flash strikes which often turn violent. Inter-union rivalries cause a power struggle among multiple unions who have different political affiliations.

Legislations affecting women employees.

The labour laws in India do suffer from many deficiencies and loopholes.

There is very little flexibility and changing the legal provisions are enormously time consuming. However, in recent times the government departments have taken care to amend laws to ensure greater benefits to women employees.

On paper the working conditions of women have improved considerably due to Maternity Benefit Amendment Act and the Sexual Harassment Acts. There are laws and rules regulating working hours, night shift for women employees, though some distinction exists for employees in factory and other establishments.

Important to note that the National capital Delhi ranks the worst for working woman according to a study by an American agency and Women participation is only 24%, which is the lowest in the world. Though many Indian states have laws, which restrict the working hours of women few states do not place any restriction.

Even in organized sector jobs women also face problems such as wage discrimination, harassment while commuting, and harassment of all forms.

A Reuter's survey placed India as the fourth most unsafe place in the world for women.

Unmarried working woman or single mom may not even get a decent place to live in Delhi and most other metros. Hate crimes and harassment of migrant working woman are rampant.

If a woman worker is to be retained beyond normal working hours, especially at night managements are required to seek appropriate exemption from the State Govt under the Shop and Establishment Act and comply with the conditions laid down by the State Govt. The compliance issues include maximum permissible working hours and overtime hours in a day or a week. This ensures undue pressure to retain woman beyond reasonable work hours. It is required of BPOs and other establishments to arrange for pick up and drop from door to door during late night shifts.

To protect the safety of women employees who commute at night, employers are required to maintain the full record of security personnel, cab drivers and of contractual workers have to be maintained, and made accessible to the police as and when required. Despite all these regulations, the crime against working woman keeps increasing.

Layoff, retrenchment or shutdown requires prior approval making it impossible to take action, even in any loss situation. Management has to give twenty-one-day notice to everyone before affecting any change in the conditions of service.

The Contract Labour (Regulation and abolition) Act of 1970 is applicable to all contractual hiring and imposes many restrictions.

The wage cost is pushed up as The Payment of Bonus Amendment Bill, 2015 proposes to bring more and more employees under bonus and to double the payments. It also proposes raising statutory bonus payments.

As per the constitution of India, states can legislate independently and few of the states have already amended the laws making it easier for management actions

Global companies must understand the peculiarities of Indian labour laws and the impact on employees' Compensation structuring. This section provides the broad details with regard to the corporate practices and the income tax implications.

One should refer to various legislations affecting the employment. HR often will encounter the question of "take home pay" from potential hires, which may actually not be easy to answer and make people understand at the time of salary negotiations.

Junior level employees would seek a higher monthly post tax pay-out and the retirement benefits do not appeal to them.

Base Pay and benefit.

The structuring of the pay and benefits can be quite a complicated affair in India. While employers have some room for flexible design of the components and offer tax-friendly pay structure to the employee, there are numerous income tax implications which choke any flexibility.

While designing particular pay for an employee, one should consider long-term and short-term financial goals of the employee. Vast majority of the candidates are unaware of the tax laws which makes pay negotiations very difficult. I have come across Software professionals asking for "take home pay" without realizing that totally depends on the tax planning by the person.

Every year the government keeps modifying the income tax rules which impact the net take-home and the retirement corpus.

Employers in India generally adopt the cost to the company CTC-concept which can be broadly divided into five categories Basic salary, Allowances, Perquisites and benefits and Retirement benefits. I would prefer a cafeteria plan, which offers flexible benefits and allows new hires to choose from a menu that has optional items. For example, the long-term superannuation plans, car expenses, may be offered as optional items. Specific needs of prospective new employee can thus be met. In a cafeteria plan, benefits required by law or by labour union contracts are not made optional or exempted. The total gross pay however is the decider. Instead of a standard one-size-fits-all benefit plans, the cafeteria plans are more difficult to administer.HR and Managements have to work extra to keep a tab of balancing the conflicting needs.

Employees may choose to change their selection and it can drive the administrative cost up.

What is as an Allowance in the pay check in India?

An allowance is the term used in India to label any financial benefit given to the employee over and above the regular basic salary.

Some of the allowances are provided to cover expenses which may be incurred during the discharge of service. Examples are medial allowance and food allowance.

It is common to give employees coupons that can be redeemed for food in choice eateries. Subsidized food in canteens also served mostly in factories.

A common one is the conveyance or transport allowance which is paid to meet expenses incurred for commuting to workplace from home.

Some organizations provide subsidized bus service.

While many of these allowances are taxable, few could be partly taxable and few others are non-taxable.

The introduction of each of the components is having a different impact on the employee's take home salary.

At the junior levels one would frequently encounter the question of take-home pay which actually is in the hands of the employee. Junior level employees would seek a higher monthly pay-out

Basic Salary: is the committed base cash component and other allowances such as the house rent allowance and Provident Fund contributions are linked to basic pay. Basic
salary or base pay is taxable.

Dearness Allowance: In India double digit inflation is common and the mechanism to address this cost of living is through Dearness Allowance. The DA is based on consumer price index and is paid typically in government jobs and not a common practice in private sector white collar jobs. It is not uncommon to find Trade unions often resorting to strike for wage revisions and on the DA formula.

Entertainment Allowance: Certain high-level executives and employees in few job roles involving customer interactions or public relations are paid a fixed amount for business promotion which may be made tax free.

Overtime Allowance: Employers provide an overtime allowance to employees working over and above the regular work hours.

City Compensatory Allowance: City Compensatory Allowance is paid to employees in urban centres, which may be highly expensive to live and to cope with the higher living costs. This allowance is fully taxable. Off late this allowance is now unpopular

Few other common fixed allowances are food allowance, medical reimbursement, telephone/mobile expenses.

Perquisites are like the sweeteners and benefits or amenities provided by the employer to an employee. The Income Tax Act allows exemption for certain perquisites.

House Rent Allowance is usually termed as HRA, which primarily addresses the urban high-cost of rented accommodation by giving tax exemption up to a limit. The house rent allowance is a taxable allowance under the Income tax Act.

Expenses of Medical treatment up to IRS 15000 per annum and transport allowance of IRS 1600 per month can be made tax free.

Uniform allowance /corporate attire are exempted to the extent of expenditure incurred up to certain limits prescribed in the Income tax act and rules.

Children's education allowance is another allowance Exempt up to Rs 100 per month for 1 children and Children hostel allowance is exempted up to Rs 300 per month for 1 child.

Professional pursuit/research allowance. Actual expenses can be claimed as exempt from tax.

Meal expenses can be claimed as exempt Rs 50 meal up to Rs 1,200 per month.

Benefits like Health club membership, GYM with sports and similar facilities can be extended to all employees to make it tax free.

A company can provide gift voucher and can be claimed as exempt up to Rs 5,000 per annum in certain tax situations.

Mobile/telephone reimbursement when provided can be exempted to the extent of actual on business calls.

To attract resources a very progressive HR message can come from allowance to buy books and periodicals which is exempt to the extent of actual expenditure

A company leased car is a major attraction as out of the total expenses incurred by the employer, only a very small portion gets taxed and attracts less tax and results in savings for the employee.

Retirement benefits:

Many senior employees are attracted by the retirement benefits; Provident fund, pension and gratuity are quite common retirement benefits extended under various social benefit laws.

Employee provident fund is contributed by employers and employee. One is allowed to withdraw at the time of retirement or for certain specified events in the life.

Provident Fund Contributions of Employer's is exempted up to twelve per cent of the salary.

The Employees' contribution is exempted along with other long-term retirement savings up to a limit specified in the Income tax.

National Pension System:

After a long period of consultation and deliberations the government introduced a pension scheme for all the central government employees except Armed Forces are the beneficiaries. The State and State Autonomous Bodies can enrol employee after a certain date. All Citizen Models" through a Point of Presence - Service Provider can be used as an alternate route to subscribe.

Corporate: Either the subscriber or the corporate can choose for investment.

The subscriber is free to choose the fund manager. The employer's contribution is exempt up to ten per cent of the salary.

Employee's contribution and the taxation:

The Employee's contribution of up to fifty thousand is tax deductible in addition to the limit of

Rs 1, 50,000. Withdrawal facilities have been changed and forty per cent of the corpus is tax-free.

Bonus:

The practice of paying bonus as profit-sharing started right from the First World War time, when certain textile mill owners started paying ten per cent of the wages for the workers as war bonus. The dictionary meaning of the word bonus is "boon or gift". The bonus paid in organizations is over and above normal wages.

In India, bonus assumes altogether different meaning, as the law makes bonus payment compulsory through The Payment of Bonus act 1965. Hence bonus assumes the nature of legal entitlement.

The Bill was passed by the Parliament on 25th September 1965 and became amended act 'The Payment of Bonus act 1965.

It aims at providing for the payment of bonus to the employees in every factory and every other establishment employing not less than twenty persons on any day during an accounting year.

The Central/State Government has also been given the power to extend it's the law to any establishment employing less than twenty but more than ten persons.

The pay limit is Rs. 10,000 per month or lower, to be given the coverage. The 2015 amendment to the act has raised this limit to IRS.21, 000 which brought more employees under the bonus benefit. The amended act made maximum bonus limit of twenty per cent of Rupees seven thousand, raising it from rupees three thousand five hundred.

A minimum of thirty days working continuously in an accounting year makes one eligible for the minimum bonus. After many years the minimum amount has been raised to higher of Rs. 583.00 or 8.33%. The Act covers a company that is in business for at least 5 years profitably and has at least 20 employees... The purpose of the act was to provide an opportunity to earn more than the minimum wages. There is legal time limit of eight months from the close of the accounting year for the payment.

The act lays down rules for calculations, payment, compliance reporting and the penalty for non-compliance. The bonus for a temporary employee is for the total number of days worked.

People employed in seasonal factories can earn proportionate bonus and not the minimum bonus as prescribed in the Act. A part-time employee is also eligible if engaged regularly.

The act is very liberal in terms of extending the benefit.

Any retrenched employee or employee under probation is eligible provided he has worked for a prescribed minimum period. Even an employee who was dismissed, but reinstated later earns the bonus. A piece rated worker is entitled to the bonus. Many court rulings validating these clarifications.

Structuring the compensation and perquisites.

A typical Indian employee 'pay would have mainly six common elements.

Base salary.

Housing related allowances.

Annual incentives or bonus

Long-term incentive plans VIZ Gratuity, Pension, Superannuation plans

Health Insurance its

Retirement benefits

Discretionary spending

Perquisites or fringe benefits

Key man insurance (mainly for senior-level executives) accident injury or death insurance benefit and medical insurance policies for self, family, and dependents.

Short-term incentives are mainly target driven and have performance criteria.

For example, the Sales personnel earn the bonus, based on targets like incremental revenue growth or the new business.

Bonuses are paid after the event and are purely discretionary. Many senior executives are given a mixture of cash and shares of the company with vesting restrictions as an added benefit.

A long-term incentive has three to five-year tenure.

It is not uncommon to extend other benefits like enhanced gratuity plans, continued health insurance post-retirement, a chauffeured limousine and interest-free loans for the purchase of a house.

In the nineties the Executive Compensation was highly regulated by Company law and there were severe constraints to the payment of salaries and commissions to the CEO. The regulations were made primarily to curb unhealthy practices of huge payments to those who had control over the company finance.

The onset of globalization has ushered in the new normal of compensation for senior executives, though the compensation of the Indian CEOs of the companies in the USA is non-comparison.

Appendix-4

India's Top Ten Highest Paid MD/CEOs

Many leading industrial houses own and controlled various business entities in their group and they had contributed significantly to the country's economic growth in India like the Tatas, Birlas, and Mahindras .They have had their business growing by leaps and bounds but the government regulated compensation and reward of key people who transformed and grew the organizations. This choked the rapid expansion and diversification attempts as there was no motivation to take risks.

The Economic control regime got reversed with liberalisation of the economy which is encouraging foreign direct investments through changes in the company law. The salaries of Indian Companies' CEOs started going up exponentially after various amendments to the Company's Act which started allowing freedom for the Board of the companies to fix the CEO's salaries.

The CEOs of public sector banks are Government appointments and hence their pay benefits are also highly restricted.

There has been over 200 per cent rise in the average salaries of CEO over the last decade. Even loss-making companies are hiring professional CEOs with top salaries.

Even the traditionally low paying companies like Larsen and Toubro, the engineering company have now started paying high salaries to the CEO

Infosys, the leading Global IT Company, paid Rupees 480 million to the CEO.

Going by the Infosys compensation history, it defies every logic about the methods adopted for the pay determination when it comes to the top position.

The company which was founded by ordinary people who lived a simple life with high morals went in for popularity rather than the competency of the candidate while deciding outsider as the CEO. They paid huge money only to quickly fire the candidate amidst scandals and go back to more reasonable pay.

Tech Mahindra is reportedly paying the highest pay package of Rupees 1500 million to the CEO.

The Banks in India which were conservative have now changed the gear to higher levels and pay

top pay. HDFC, ICICI bank started the trend with top-end pay. Hero Motor Corporation, Lupin laboratory pay around fifty million to their CEO.

References

Alfie Kohn, "Penalizing by Rewards-The trouble with gold stars, Incentive plans, A's, Praises and other bribes" Amazon, 1999.

Brookshire Bethany, "Dopamine –Is it love, Gambling, Reward, Or Addiction?" The State of the Universe, July 3, 2013.

Cherry Kendra, "Left brain VS right brain Dominance; the surprising Truth", Psychology; 6 September, 2016

Crawford, LePine Rich, "Linking job demands, and resources to employee engagement and burnout: a theoretical extension and meta-analytic test", Journal of Applied Psychology, 2010.

Dan Pink, "The surprising science of motivation", YouTube.

Dean, Emily, "Dopamine Primer", "How Dopamine makes us human", Psychology Today, 13 May 2011.

Deci Edward L Koestner, Richard; Ryan, Richard M. "A meta-analytic review of experiments examining the effects of extrinsic rewards on intrinsic motivation". Psychological Bulletin, Vol 125 (6), Nov 1999, 627-668.

DeShon, Richard P; Gillespie, Jennifer Z.A, "Motivated Action Theory Account of Goal Orientation", Journal of Applied Psychology, Vol 90(6), Nov 2005, 1096-1127.

Dill Kathryn, "The Best Places to Work in 2016", Forbes, December 14, 2015.

Elliot, Andrew J, Harackiewicz, Judith M "Goal setting, achievement orientation, and intrinsic motivation: A meditational analysis." Journal of Personality and Social Psychology, Vol 66 (5), May 1994, 968-980.

ELM expertise on labour mobility, "3 Main Differences in Management Culture between the US and China", May 10, 2011.Franco E. Santos, "Rewards and Punishments: The role of operant conditioning in human behaviour"-Comment B.F. Skinner, classical conditioning; February 26, 2015.

Freek Vermeulen, "Breaking Bad Habits: Defy Industry Norms and Reinvigorate Your Business", Harvard Business Review Press, 2017.

One More Time: "How Do You Motivate Employees?" Harvard Business Review, January- February 1968.

Gauthier Bradley, "Psychology Concepts for improving employee Motivations, New Methods organization, Psychology Concepts," August 17.2011.

George D Shaw, "The pros and cons of ESOPs" CFO.COM, 28 January 2013.

Gillian B. White, "The Opioid Crisis Comes to the Workplace", the Atlantic, October, 3, 2017.

Hardeep Matharu, Independent, "Employers in Sweden introduce six-hour work day", 1 October 2016.

Henderson, Richard L. Compensation Management in a Knowledge-Based World. 9th ed. Upper Saddle River, NJ: Prentice-Hall, 2003.

James R. Lincoln, Arne L, Kalleberg, "Culture, Control, and Commitment: A Study of Work Organization and Work."

Konstan, David, "Epicurus", the Stanford Encyclopaedia of Philosophy

(Fall 2016 Edition), Edward N. Zalta (Ed.).

Leadership at Work, 6 Ed. New York: McGraw-Hill, 1996.

Loren Rodgers, "The Employee Ownership Update", National Centre for employee ownership, January 3, 2017.

Mary C Lamia, "Intense Emotions and Strong Feelings", Psychology Today, November 20, 2011.

Markus McGill, "What is oxytocin and what does it do?" Medical News Today, 21, September 2015.

Matt Levine, "This Is How Much Every Lehman Brothers IBD Associate, VP, And Senior VP Got Paid In 2007", Bonus Watch 2007.

Michael Armstrong, Helen Murlis, "Reward Management" Hogan Page 5th edition.

Ormrod Jeanne, Human learning 6th edition.

Peter Conti-Brown, "Why Wells Fargo Might Not Survive Its Fake Accounts Scandal", Fortune, August 31, 2017

Rev Ezekiel, A. Ajibade, "African Traditional Work Ethics and the challenges of decent work agenda", Journal of International Business Studies, March 1997, Volume 28, Issue 1, 177–207.

Stars Richard M, Lyman W; Porter and Gregory A; Bigley "Driving force and Leadership at Work." 6th Ed. New York: McGraw-Hill, 1996.

Suri Dhruv, "Do you understand how your ESOPs work?" You're Story, 12, September, 2015.

Tommy Tomlinson, Precious memories, ESPN, 5 March 2014.

The Economic Times, July 4, 2016.

Wolfsdorf, David, "Pleasure in Ancient Greek Philosophy", Cambridge University Press.2013.

About the Author:

Dr. E. J. Sarma is a strategic management consultant specializing in Organizational Change Management and Human Resource Management. He has been training, mentoring employees and executives for leadership skills in a global environment. He has written over 200 articles in leading journals. He is the author of the book on Change management. He has been a practicing HR executive for over 35 years in Global organizations. He has a PhD and MBA in Business Administration from Mumbai University.

www.ingramcontent.com/pod-product-compliance
Lightning Source LLC
Chambersburg PA
CBHW031628210526
45464CB00004B/1794